Business
Fitness

Business Fitness

The Power to Succeed–*Your* Way

Dawn G. Lennon

Glenbridge Publishing Ltd.

Published by Glenbridge Publishing Ltd.
19923 E. Long Ave.
Centennial, Colorado 80016

Library of Congress Catalog Card Number: LC: 2006939842

International Standard Book Number: 978-0-944435-63-2

10 9 8 7 6 5 4 3 2 1

For Dad,

who faced every adversity
with wisdom, optimism, wit, and love

Michael W. Galloway
(1920-1994)

"Not one word spoke he more than was needed…
And gladly would he learn and gladly teach."

The Clerk from Geoffrey Chaucer's,
The Canterbury Tales

Table of Contents

Acknowledgments

Words are intimate and beloved companions just like the wonderful people who have shared the kind and encouraging words I have leaned on while writing this book. I am always amazed at how the faith of others can buoy our faith in ourselves.

I am especially grateful for the constant encouragement from my brother, Doug, and for the intellectual energy that my friend, Karin Costello, generates in me every time we talk—and that's often! Thanks also to my mother, Dixie, and sister, Dale, for always being in my corner.

I am uniquely grateful to Gene Witiak, V.M.D., who invited me to edit his book in 2004, an experience that prepared me for my own efforts. His words and his confidence inspired me.

There are many who have showed their support along the way by either reading portions of the manuscript or offering insights, but special thanks go to Tom Stathos, Lee Crago, Drew Maron, Annette Gardner, Alicia Orbin, Diane Donaher, Jeff Focht, and Suzanne Fidler.

The course of my professional career was set by three gentlemen who saw something in me that I didn't. If it were not for their willingness to take a chance on me, my professional life would have been very different. So my heartfelt gratitude remains with Don Langlois, Art Van Horn, and Merl Hertzog.

To all of you who take the time to read all or part of this book, I thank you too. I hope that you will be inspired to increase your career options and success by becoming business fit.

D.G.L.

PART ONE

BUSINESS FITNESS

Chapter 1

EXACTLY WHAT KIND OF SUCCESS
DO YOU WANT?

When I was in the sixth grade, I remember being
in a girls' gym class on a day when we were going to play
kickball. In those days I was a chubby girl, athletic
enough, reasonably competitive, and fun-loving. The
other girls liked me, so when it came time for the team
captains to start selecting their teammates, I was picked
early.

I stood next to my captain and watched as each
successive girl was chosen. First it was the most popular
girls, then the ones who were plain, and lastly the unfit
and unusual. Big surprise! But as a twelve-year-old, I

remember feeling very sad and also very lucky. I thought how awful I would feel to be chosen last, to feel unwanted and less valued. I realized that what I'd really wanted was what I got—to be recognized for my worth and then to take on the game's challenge with my peers. As a preadolescent, I saw success as having the captain choose me over others. I still think about those girls picked last and wonder how they would have defined success on that day—maybe it was just surviving the discomfort of the moment, not being the very last one chosen, or managing their hurt with dignity.

If anything has stuck with me from this experience, it's this:

It is generally better to be in a position to choose than to be chosen.

Unfortunately, choosing isn't always as simple as it looks. It assumes that you clearly know what you want and what you don't want. The emphasis here is on *you*.

Consider those kickball team captains. Both were in a position to pick the best players and to gain a competitive edge. They just needed to figure out who the most capable players were and then pick as many of them as they could. But what if one of those captains was new to the class and hadn't seen those girls play before? What if the other captain was under pressure to select her friends first because that was how she proved her loyalty? What if the best players didn't like the captains and selecting them would mean conflict on the team? So choosing often comes down to expedience, meeting the expectations of others, or just a stab in the dark.

Our struggle with choice starts early in life and never lets up. It doesn't take long for us as children to learn the basics of a business transaction. When we do something that adults like, we position ourselves for reward; when we do things that adults don't like, we experience undesirable consequences. The older we get the more we realize that similar transactions can yield very different results. For instance, when we are toddlers and get a boo-boo that makes us cry, we are likely to get fussed over and cuddled until we calm down. If the same thing happens when we are ten years old, crying over a minor hurt can get us a scolding for being a baby. As a result, we become more sophisticated about our behavioral choices so we can get the reactions that we want from others. Our personal behavioral choices are something *we* control; it's those marketplace choices that become a challenge.

From the time we are very young, we learn that we need money to pay for the things we want and the things other people have that we think we ought to want. From a child's point of view, having stuff is a measure of success. It becomes pretty clear very soon that some of our friends have more stuff than we do and that must mean something, although we're just not sure what. It also becomes clear that material things are somehow linked to having a job, and a job is something we get from someone else.

As kids, we may have gotten our first jobs from our parents like taking out the trash, mowing the lawn, or cleaning our rooms for which there was some kind of reward. When we became teenagers, those jobs might have come from fast food restaurants, retail stores, or warehouses. In adulthood there were likely a chain of different jobs—some good and some awful. For some people there were jobs just for paychecks and for others there were jobs that led to growth careers. No matter what the job, it always came from an employer who chose us to do particular work for specific payment. Getting hired is a lot like being selected for the kickball team.

Looking for a job is one of those uncomfortable economic requirements of life that most people face with dread. In all likelihood, at some point in the process, we feel like those last few girls being picked for the kickball team—unfit, unusual, and unwanted. We always talk about "looking" for a job like it's a colored egg that the Easter Bunny has hidden in the shrubbery. "Looking" for a job means trying to find someone who will choose you to work for them. You apply for their job and they accept or reject you. In reality both parties are actually looking for each other—you're looking for the right job to position you for the success you want, and the employer finds and hires you to achieve desired business results. The process just never feels that mutual, primarily because of the way we tend to approach it.

Most people who look for a job don't have a clue about what they're really looking for. Sometimes they just want some business to employ them so that the nagging questions about why they aren't working will stop. They often accept positions because the title sounds important, the money is better than what they earned before, or it meets family approval. People find it either overwhelming or just plain scary to spend time figuring out what they really want from employment.

The truth is that jobs exist to serve businesses and bring them success. Jobs are maintained or created because a business needs work to be done for a variety of reasons: to launch a product or service, to maintain revenue and cash flow, to keep things running smoothly, to increase profitability, or to grow. A business doesn't invent a job because there are people like us in the marketplace who need a paycheck. Jobs are added or retained because they will contribute to the success of the business, namely its profitability. If we happen to come along and seem to fit the requirements of a job, we may land it—but then again, we may not. The business makes that choice, not us. It's not personal—it's business.

Successful businesses clearly understand the needs they fill in the marketplace and who their customers are. They are focused on what they need to do to compete effectively and ethically to remain profitable and to grow. You too are a business—albeit a business of one. Your capabilities are the product or service that you want to position in the marketplace—those capabilities are the basis from which you can grow your own success. If you don't know exactly what kind of success you want and don't know how to define and direct your strengths to find that success, you will tend to make choices in a vacuum.

It's common knowledge that to be a successful athlete at any level, you have to understand how to play the game strategically and tactically. You also must have the physical skills to be competitive and the mental toughness to win regardless of the circumstances. Successful athletes, whether they are shortstops, golfers, quarterbacks, or point guards, commit themselves totally to the disciplines of their sport. They develop a level of physical and mental fitness that prepares them to handle any new direction in the game, any challenge by the opponent, and any scoring pressure. The great ones build muscle memory, game savvy, and steeled nerves, waiting for and seizing that critical moment to put away the contest decisively. Standout athletes learn how to win early on and then build an unshakable foundation of knowledge, strength, and skill that sustains them throughout their athletic careers and into the future. This model works as beautifully in business as it does on the field, the links, the gridiron, or the court with no need for ankle tapings, protective padding, or rubdowns.

Business fitness positions you to do the choosing.

In the marketplace the successful players achieve a level of business fitness that gives them the knowledge and skill that they need to achieve desired business results and the mental toughness to handle pressures and stresses under fire. Being business fit means developing intellectual strength and steady nerves so that you are positioned to handle any circumstance at anytime, anywhere. This doesn't mean that, if you are business fit, you will hit a home run in every difficult business situation; it simply means that you will have enough understanding, insight, composure and savvy to hold your own in a business discussion, negotiation, or transaction. It can buy you time. When you are business fit, you understand clearly the outcome you want and what it means to you and the business. You are aware of the expectations of the stakeholders; you appreciate the risks and trade-offs that are in your line of sight; and you know where to go to get the support, information, and resources you need to make the right things happen. Business fitness means that you are well fortified to make the best choices at the moment—ones that move you toward the success that you want.

Success Is About You. It's That Simple

If someone asked, "How will you know when you are successful in your work life," what would you say? If they asked, "How far are you from achieving the success you want," what would your answer be? If they asked, "How are you going to achieve that success," how would you describe your plan?

These are straightforward questions that can be very difficult to answer. Sometimes the best you can do is offer an answer composed of bits and pieces but that's a start. Big picture questions require long-range thinking. They require you to look into yourself and read the crystal ball of your own life. Sometimes the picture you see inside starts out cloudy, then there is a little bit of clearing when you look again, and finally certain images get clear and stay clear. It is a growth process. This kind of searching requires you to tolerate ambiguity and uncertainty even as you are presented with opportunities that require you to make important work-life choices. But that's the adventure of it all. If you don't venture out, you'll never discover anything.

It is not unusual to start out seeking success in one direction and then change course. We quickly learn in life that things are rarely what they seem. Certain jobs may not be as glamorous as they seem, starting your own business not as straightforward as it seems, managers not as committed to customers as they seem, or employees not as satisfied with their jobs as they seem. As a result, it is important to accept the fact that the path to success is not as straight as it may seem. If you ask successful people to describe the chronology of their work lives, you will likely hear about a lot of side trips along the way, but the characteristics of their destinations were always clear.

Getting clear about what success means to you is a lot like building a healthy meal from a sumptuous buffet. Figuring out the kind of success that will satisfy you throughout your life means identifying your options and customizing them to your needs and obligations. Success indicators tend to fall into three categories: financial, experiential/positional, and personal. For some people success centers within one of these three categories and for others there is a mix. The chart below is a short list of success indicators that provide a starting point for your thinking. Take some time to explore those that apply to you, tailor them so they work for you, and add other factors. Thinking now about your success indicators will prepare you to dig into the seven smart moves of business fitness to get you there in Parts II and III.

PERSONAL SUCCESS INDICATORS

Financial	Experiential/ Positional	Personal
Live debt free	Hold an executive position	Nurture family/ friends
Build many income streams	Manage/lead others	Serve the community
Amass real estate holdings	Get unique assignments	Engage in charity work
Earn a six-figure income	Pursue formal education	Pursue hobbies/ sports
Build investments	Travel	Deepen spirituality
Live within your means	Achieve expertise/ mastery	Increase confidence
Accumulate "toys"	Become an entrepreneur	Build good self-esteem
Build discretionary income	Achieve recognition	Protect your health
Achieve social status	Mentor others	Find love and belonging

As tempting as it is to think about success only in singular terms, the reality is that our individual success is often tied to the success of the business that employs us. If you are an entrepreneur, the connection between your personal success indicators and those of your business is likely very close. If you work for an organization, the relationship between what you do and how your business responds should be evident and immediate. Since the 1990s it has become clearer to the corporate workforce that "big business" lives or dies by the performance of the people who work there. Sometimes the success-failure scale is tipped by the decisions and ethics of senior leaders, sometimes by the economic demands or capabilities of the workforce, and other times by dramatic shifts in the marketplace. More often than not, our long-term individual success and the success of the business are mutually dependent. Arguably, successful businesses are those that employ people whose concept of individual success aligns with business success. That's why it is so important to make choices that position you in the right job in the right business at the right time, so you can help optimize mutual success.

It doesn't matter whether you are a business owner, the CEO, a department manager, first-line supervisor, staff professional, or frontline worker; there are business success indicators that you can support. After all, you are an arm of the business that employs you and, like it or not, contribute to its image for good or ill. As you build your personal business fitness, you contribute to the strengthening of the business you work for. Here is a short list of Business Success Indicators that will help you to help your business increase its own business fitness.

BUSINESS SUCCESS INDICATORS

Fiscal	Leadership	Social
Profitability	Positive industry example	Support employee causes
Controlled growth	Loyal customers	Serve the community
Convertible assets	Innovative culture	Give to charities
Well-paid employees	A learning organization	Sponsor key events
Secure pension fund	High standards of integrity	Lead social initiatives

Managed costs	Exceptional quality	Be politically active
Consistent dividends	Committed employees	Be visible
Reinvestment capital	Public recognition	Be represented on Boards
Good benefits	Collaboration	Mentor

Achieving success for yourself and your business requires attention, effort, patience, and perseverance. It is important to remember this:

Your work life is neither a contest nor a race— it is an unfolding.

Too many people want to believe that the events of life are linear simply because we tend to be chronologically oriented. Our daily life is typically driven by units of time. Everyday we wake up at the appointed hour, get dressed, go to work and then to school sporting events, have dinner, do chores, read or watch TV, and go to bed exhausted from the pressures of the clock. We tend to think of our lives as a continuum that goes like this: graduate from school, get a job, get married, buy a house, have children, hang on to that job for dear life or find a better job, rear the children, marry or see them off; then retire to travel, eat out, and play golf until you gasp your last breath.

Although this sounds like a tidy plan, for many it plays out like this: graduate from school, struggle to get a first job, look for something better, get married, find another job, have children, buy a house, go back to school to add credentials, and make a lateral job move.

Then move into a bigger house, sadly get divorced, share custody of the children, start dating again, look for a better paying job, get the kids through school and out on their own. Finally, settle down with a new life partner, work until your company lets you go with a package, and then retire to travel, eat out, and play golf until you gasp your last breath.

Life is full of surprises—some good and some not so good. If we turn our options over to a precut, subconscious system, then we'll often get a disappointing and colorless result. Remember when you were a kid and adults would ask you, "Now, what do you want to be when you grow up?" I do. My answer was that I wanted to be a farmer, Annie Oakley, and a forest ranger. People thought that was cute, but it didn't take long for me to get the message that girls didn't do those kinds of things. When I was a kid, most girls who sought careers were expected to "want" to be secretaries, nurses, or teachers. So I became a high school teacher because it was a respectable profession, I wanted to be in service to others, and I received a lot of positive reinforcement, affirmation, and validation for my choice. I was a dedicated and successful teacher for a decade, but that little voice was still whispering a desire for an agrarian life. The pathetic sound of that voice became so faint that the conditions had to be just right or I couldn't hear it.

It is very easy to turn down the volume on that inner voice. Sometimes others shut it off for us, and sometimes we do it ourselves. For a lucky few, the volume is deafening; for others the whisper struggles for a hearing. Either by intention or by default we are all headed somewhere. Events occur around us that force us to make conscious or unconscious choices that directly affect our next steps. We are presented with paths to take that determine how we live: Do we commit ourselves to a sedentary life or an active one? Do we participate actively in the lives of our family members, or do we leave that to our spouse? Do we expand our skills, knowledge, and experiences so that we can grow in our work life, or do we just take the path of least resistance? Do we pursue interesting hobbies where we meet new people, maybe even people unlike ourselves, so that we widen our understanding of other cultures and perspectives? These are the kinds of choices that are presented to us. Not choosing is a choice, so there is never anyone but our own self to blame for the way things turn out.

We are the product of our choices.

Making good choices is a function of understanding what you want and the probability of that choice getting it for you, in whole or in part. Choice gives you control; it also gives you accountability for outcomes, both good and bad. In that equation, the likelihood of you achieving success in your life comes from maximizing your opportunities.

You can let your life unfold without having a hand in it, or you can be an active participant. Business fitness is the platform from which to orchestrate both your personal and business life choices. It is a model that positions you to devise a flexible plan that leads you to the kind of success you want throughout your lifetime. It delivers an organic set of results one step at a time.

The Way You Start Affects the Way You Finish

Success in the business world is not about you winning and someone else losing. If you start out on a journey toward success without a clear picture of what you are pursuing, then what you get in the end will be some default result. You might like that result or you might not. Either way you have nothing to complain about since you had no particular direction in the first place.

Some people are career-oriented and others are job-oriented. Pursuing a career means committing up front to a skills, knowledge, and experience growth process in the marketplace. For example, if you want to pursue a career in computer technology, your career path might go like this: Earn a B.S. degree in computer science and take a series of programming and systems maintenance jobs. Become supervisor of software training, then manager of hardware installations, director of systems integration, and Chief Information Officer. You might have to work for a couple of companies to build your skills and capabilities, but if the success you want is an executive position, this is one path to the corner office. By pursuing a systematic plan to broaden your capabilities and increase your business value over time, you position yourself to attain the level of achievement and recognition that you want.

If you are job-oriented, your emphasis is on achieving excellence in a specific area of interest. Let's say you are very good at product sales—a great work life fit for you. You have excelled at product sales jobs in all kinds of industries from the time you graduated from school—selling sneakers at the local sporting goods store, new and used cars for a regional dealership, and grocery products for a national distributor. Each of these jobs improved your income, honed your sales skills, and increased your knowledge of the product sales industry. By building expertise around a specific skill that you excel in, you can position yourself for the success that you want.

However, there is another, less desirable job-orientation profile that I call "job stacking." It goes like this: Graduate from school and get a job in an office doing various administrative duties. Find out about another office job that pays more and take that job. Learn some software applications on the job that you master quickly. Take some courses on new software and implement those programs at work. Go to another company that needs your new capabilities and offers better benefits.

At the new company you discover that the salary for a customer service phone representative is higher than yours, so you transfer to that department. There you learn how to handle customer calls and use the call distribution software. Then you decide after a couple years that the higher pay isn't worth the stress and the captive nature of this work. Your existing software skills, however, are no longer current and don't align with what you want to do. Your options have become limited. You don't know what to do next, so you stay on the phones. This is the scenario when you string together jobs without a plan. You end up with a default career that increasingly reduces your options for growth.

An entrepreneur caught in this pattern is inclined to start and fold one business after another, never achieving sustainable success. Or he or she will routinely change product and service lines to meet temporary market demands, confusing and frustrating his/her customer base.

This is why knowing what kind of success you want at the beginning can, after a fashion, predict the end. If you know where you are ultimately headed, you will make choices that pull you in that direction. If not, you are likely to do what is expedient with little awareness of where it may lead.

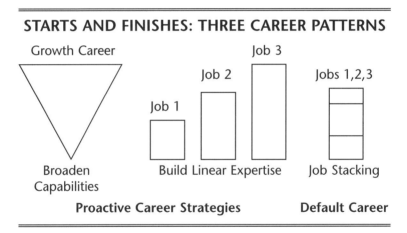

STARTS AND FINISHES: THREE CAREER PATTERNS

Growth Career

Broaden Capabilities

Job 1

Job 2

Job 3

Build Linear Expertise

Jobs 1,2,3

Job Stacking

Proactive Career Strategies   **Default Career**

Where and how you start on the path to the success has a palpable impact on where and how you finish. Just look around and you will see extraordinary examples of people who have made their way to a successful business life—and often a satisfying personal life.

Introducing the Cast of Characters

At the end of this chapter I'll introduce you to my "cast of characters" for this book—people whose stories of success or trial will reappear, illustrating how the essentials of business fitness apply in a variety of settings and circumstances.

These are all real people whom I have known and who for a variety of reasons will remain anonymous. I have given them fictitious names connecting them to quandaries or the businesses they were in; hopefully, that will help you to keep them straight when they appear in future chapters. Some have achieved the level of success that they wanted, which may be more or less than what you want. That doesn't matter. It's the way they went about things that is important; their stories are simply visual reference points for you. There are others who had success and lost it, stunned and confused by what happened, and unprepared for the aftermath.

As your narrator for these individual histories, you should know that I have enormous admiration and regard for the resilience of people in life, especially in business situations. As good people succeed or fail, they generally demonstrate a unique valor. It heartens me when perseverance and effort are rewarded. It pains me to see collapse when there were opportunities to avoid it. Each story starts by looking at the kind of success that was pursued and ends with what was achieved.

A Crooked Path May Be Straighter Than You Think

I confessed earlier that as a child I wanted to grow up to be a farmer, Annie Oakley, and a forest ranger. I loved animals, the outdoors, the freedom of spirit that hard physical work gave me, and the inspiring beauty of nature. But I needed to make a living when I got older, so I became an English teacher—which was the perfect first career for me. It also was an incubator for the evolution of my management skills. As a teacher, I had to plan and organize lessons, establish performance standards and evaluate assignments, set and enforce rules, handle conflict, solve problems, make decisions, and manage political situations, namely parent concerns and administrative directives.

After ten years in education, I realized that I was no longer increasing my own skills or testing myself, so I began to explore job options in the largest companies in my region. I spent several weeks talking with area businesses about the impacts of poor communication skills in the workplace. That gave me a comfort level with corporate towers and men in three-piece suits with which I was unfamiliar. By some manner of luck, my résumé found its way to another company where I was eventually hired.

I spent twenty-two years there in key management positions in marketing, consumer programs, human resources, customer service, quality, and change management. Nearly all of my bosses were VPs, so I was exposed to high-level strategic and operational planning from the outset. Needless to say, these opportunities cultivated big picture thinking, expanded my skills, and provided leadership positions from which I could have a positive impact on employees and customers. But the blue sky and green grass was always outside my office window instead of over my head and under my feet, so I wasn't as happy as I needed to be.

I started to feel constrained by the requirements of corporate life. So I bought a farm and set up a horse breeding operation—both of which I knew nothing about. Using the business skills that I had accumulated over the years, I created a modest horse business that challenged me in ways that I had never imagined. As tough and frustrating as it was, it renewed me. I learned that what I really wanted was to be free and independent each day of my life to dedicate myself to the things I loved doing.

So as soon as I reached early retirement age, I left the security of the big corporation that had been so good to me. I walked away from the nice salary that came every two weeks like clockwork and all of the prestige that came from working for a well-respected Fortune 500 company. What I walked toward was a lifestyle that let me build an organic relationship between my personal interests and my work life. From this platform, I started a business consulting practice focused on helping individuals and businesses solve problems and improve performance.

My own crooked path demonstrates how an awareness of your personal success factors from the start sets you up for the finish that you want. As you read about the seven business fitness moves, you'll see how they can help you find the success you want.

In a Nutshell

If you want to achieve independence in your work life, you need to maximize your options and position yourself to make choices that bring you the success that *you* really want.

It always pays to look before you leap in business, being sure that what you're leaping toward is something that you truly want. If you are prepared and ready before you act, you position yourself to maximize your opportunities for success. Chapter 2 gives you the details.

The Cast of Characters: Beginnings and Endings

The Perils of Hanging On: The Story of Matt Clinger

Matt Clinger was a high-ranking manager in a large corporation in the 1970s, well connected with executive management. He and some company VPs would periodically do some heavy partying in the evenings, and Matt would at times need to drive some seriously inebriated executives home though he wasn't in very good shape himself. Matt considered himself part of the "in" crowd with a very secure job.

Matt Clinger had a photographic memory and could remember and recite company minutia in a heartbeat. This made him a kind of walking company encyclopedia; however, he had difficulty decoupling himself from those details when he was called upon to offer strategic insights—the fare of his higher ranking colleagues.

More than anything Matt wanted to retire comfortably to a shoreline getaway. As long as he could please executive management, he felt safe. The problem was that this cadre of executives started changing. Suddenly, he wasn't an insider anymore. All his old buddies had left the company. He was now reporting to a strategically-oriented, hard-driving man who had no patience for minutia. Matt couldn't adjust. Gradually, he was sidelined, his scope of responsibility significantly reduced, and his office moved to an out-of-sight, out-of-mind location. In time Matt was downsized, well before he was ready to make his retirement move. Sadly, he died two years later.

Matt Clinger's idea of success was to settle into a cradle-to-grave corporate system, collecting its fruits in terms of annual salary increases, good benefits, and a secure position. He was waiting for the years to go by, watching his money grow along the way, and anticipating a long retirement without a care in the world. In today's marketplace this strategy is a lot like playing casino slot machines—you might win here and there but most of the time you lose. The difference between gambling a pocketful of quarters and your lifetime, however, is huge.

It's More Than Appearances: The Story of Hal Dodger

Hal Dodger was a well-meaning and courteous man who started with his company right out of college. He worked in a rural location where people were generally low-key and hard working. Hal had a service job that required him to work with local community leaders and contractors. He worked in that location for about fifteen years.

It came as a surprise to his colleagues when Hal relocated to the company's administrative offices in a small city some distance away where he researched external trends. He held that job for about a year until he was reassigned—reason unstated. In his next position, Hal needed to work with line and staff management to improve their performance capabilities.

Hal always came to work on time, dressed professionally, carried a briefcase, and seemed very organized. He called on clients, met with peers, and attended meetings. Soon there was a groundswell of complaints from his clients and colleagues. He never delivered any results. His clients started to avoid him, and his peers railed because he didn't pull his weight.

Hal needed to succeed at work because he had a young family. However, he simply didn't have the acumen and skills to do the work assigned to him or the ability to build the kind of relationships he needed to get things done. He was ultimately fired for poor performance and never questioned the validity of the company's decision. He just couldn't believe on an emotional level that it was really happening to him. For all those years, he had been dodging the fact that he couldn't do the work.

To Hal success meant looking and playing the part, having a respectable position at a good company, and associating with prominent people. Hal never pursued what he really wanted in life—a public school teaching career. He became what others wanted him to be so he could warrant their esteem. If he would have been let go in his twenties rather than in his forties, he might have had a legitimate shot at that career. Sometimes losing your job gets you to the path you should be on. But for Hal, that didn't happen.

Look Before You Leap: The Story of Cliff Black

Cliff Black ran a major plant operation for a large company in a remote but beautiful location. He enjoyed lots of freedom to manage his organization with little central office interference. It was a tightly knit group of mostly men, truly like a family. He was treated by his employees and the community like an executive, albeit without the title. The executive to whom he reported held Cliff in high regard.

Cliff had about five years to go before he could take retirement. It seemed that he had achieved all the success that he'd ever wanted. One day, much to his surprise, Cliff was contacted by his executive boss and offered a promotion—a chance to be a vice president for one of the company's district offices. Clearly, this offer was meant to reward him for his years of capable service to the company. He was quick to accept the offer. Cliff's employees were sad to see him go.

The employees at his new post did little to make him feel welcome. Cliff faced some extraordinary challenges as a district vice president, principally since he had no real understanding of the role he was expected to play. It didn't take long before these pressures took their toll. First it was doctor visits and then extended time off for stress-related illness. When he returned to work, he was unable to function well. One day he collapsed at work and was taken away in an ambulance. Not long after, Cliff Black went on medical leave and later was granted early retirement.

Cliff is not unlike many people who, when offered a promotion, grab it. After all, we think that if the company offers us a new job, the leadership must know that we can do it. So without thinking about our personal success indicators, we say "yes" and take our chances. Cliff thought that if he could run one area of the company, he could run another. He was likely intoxicated by those words "vice president" and the implied power and prestige the position connoted. Cliff paid a dear price for that.

Get Started and Keep Going: The Story of Julia Masters

When Julia Masters graduated from high school, she immediately got a job in the steno pool for a large, solid corporation offering salary and benefits that were very attractive. She had no real understanding of what her career options were, especially since she only had a high school diploma, but she knew she was smart, always produced quality work, and made a good impression on everyone around her. So for a while she was comfortable and safe in her role.

One day her boss asked her about her career plans. Julia mentioned that she was interested in accounting, but when asked why she hadn't gone on to college, Julia didn't have much of an answer. In fact she simply hadn't imagined herself in a professional career and wasn't sure if she could cut it in college. But the seed was planted, and in time Julia got up the nerve to start taking undergraduate courses that were reimbursed by the company.

One successful course outcome led to another over many years until Julia received her B.S. degree and a new sense of what she could accomplish. Company managers noticed her stick-to-itiveness and her energy level, especially as she applied for various posted positions. She wasn't afraid to move in new directions, especially technology. Managers were willing to take a chance on her because she had taken a chance on herself. Although she had plenty of doubts about her capabilities, she wasn't going to let them hold her back.

Julia's career risk-taking momentum was building up steam. She believed she needed an M.B.A. to position her for other career moves, so she again went to school nights to attain it. That got her noticed anew and landed her a complex and demanding management position with a staff of seasoned professionals not at all ready to accept her. There was no schooling that would help her through the internal strife of gaining the respect of her staff. So she sought out successful leaders who mentored her and their guidance worked. Julia drew on her experiences and allies to meet new leadership challenges. She became a savvy corporate professional because she challenged herself to get started and kept growing at every stage of her career.

Stop the Bleeding: The Story of Dr. Barker

Dr. Barker was a dedicated veterinarian who cared as much about people as he did about critters. After working as a staff doctor at a prominent local veterinary practice, Dr. B opened his own, full-service veterinary hospital—employees, pharmacy, surgery, x-ray, and hospitalization—the works! Dr. Barker had a great way with his clients who loved him. He was friendly and funny, committed and thorough, generous with his time, and fair with his fees.

Dr. Barker also expected his staff to be as dedicated and sharp about the needs of the animals, the clients, and the practice as he was, and most of them were. The practice was growing rapidly, requiring more and more business direction around inventory, employee policies, hiring, training, and communication. While Dr. B was focusing on medicine and pet care, the back-office practice functions were showing symptoms of internal decline.

Amid the demands of a steady stream of people, pets, and practice problems, Dr. B's office manager, Jeanette, quit. The practice had lost its administrative backbone and was now adrift. Jeanette's leaving was a watershed moment for Dr. Barker.

Dr. Barker quickly arranged to meet with Janette, listening carefully to her concerns and frustrations. He promised to make changes and involve her. He realized that he didn't know how to fix things—he was a well-trained veterinarian but an untrained businessman.

So Dr. Barker hired a veterinary practice management consultant who worked with him and Jeanette to correct problems and address discontent. Dr. B. committed himself to learning management skills that were foreign to him even though it made him uncomfortable at first. He led by example and others followed.

Dr. Barker chose to take his personal business limitations seriously and to acknowledge their potential impact on his employees. His years of success were a well-earned reward for his caring, courage, and continuous effort.

The Proof Is in the Pudding: The Story of Bert and Lee Cook

Bert and Lee Cook were educators with a flare for the arts and entertaining. Each had an inviting personal style that was warm and adventuresome. The Cooks had spent most of their professional lives with students in the classroom and as advisors for after-school activities.

The Cooks loved to entertain—Lee was a terrific gourmet cook and Bert the expert host. Nothing satisfied them more than inviting people into their home and creating a unique and upbeat dining event. Even so, it came as something of a surprise to friends when the Cooks announced that they were opening an upscale, gourmet restaurant. Neither one had ever owned a business. Neither one knew anything about the restaurant business. No matter, they left their secure teaching jobs and ventured out.

They put together a quality, though limited, menu to start. They hired former students as waiters and waitresses. They invited their friends to openings and parties there and then held their breath. Word traveled fast that the Cook's restaurant was different—interesting food, a feeling that you were dining at a friend's house, entertaining conversations with the owners, and limited seatings. Bert and Lee decided that they didn't want to become engulfed by the rigors of the restaurant business, so they limited the days and hours of operation. That was over twenty years ago and their business has been a continuous success.

Success for the Cooks started with the approval of their customers who praised their luscious appetizers, entrées, and desserts. As customers continued to return and bring their friends, Bert and Lee started becoming a kind of extended family for many of their patrons. It was the quality of the Cook's cuisine and the warmth of their establishment that brought them the success that they wanted.

Keep Your Eye on the Prize: The Story of Doug Hart

Doug Hart was a high-energy guy with a charismatic personality and tons of drive. He had a clear view of what he wanted to achieve in his career from the time he graduated from college. He wanted to have enough money by the time he was forty-five so he didn't have to work for anyone else again unless he wanted to. So off Doug went into the world of business.

He had a B.A. degree in business administration but couldn't find work that interested him. In time he got a job at a suburban hospital where he met a cardiologist who helped him become an operating room technician specializing in heart catheterizations. Doug worked at the hospital for a number of years, fully aware that his salary there wasn't going to get him to his financial goals unless he became a doctor. That wasn't in the cards. He realized that his operating room expertise, growing knowledge of heart catheterizations, and his business acumen were very attractive to companies selling new heart care technology to doctors. He was pursued by a number of these firms and eventually signed on with one of them.

Doug had no prior experience with product sales but he had a natural affinity for it. What he wasn't prepared for was the intense competition of the industry. Sales guys came and went; the corporate heads were high-pressure and tough as nails. Doug was in the midst of people who were in the game to make serious money. It took some getting used to for Doug who, despite his personal quest for a big nest egg, would never run over someone to get it. In time Doug learned how to succeed in the sales game but on his terms—demonstrating his value to the company and dealing fairly with his doctor clients.

Doug is a true example of the value of understanding what kind of success you really want. He didn't know *how* he was going to achieve his goal when he was in his twenties, but he knew what his goal was and never compromised it. Doug remained flexible, always tried to understand the impact of his choices, drew on the advice and example of others, and stayed the course. The result was a dream that came true with plenty of extras.

YOUR SUCCESS INVENTORY

Achieving success starts with knowing what you really want and where you are in the process of getting it. Your success indicators become the conscious or unconscious drivers for the choices that you make. Your responses on this inventory will become an important reference point as you move through the essentials of business fitness and will contribute to your ultimate action plan.

Describe briefly the career/job you've always dreamed of but have *never* seriously pursued.

List three ways your current career/job aligns with your "dream" job?

1.

2.

3.

List three desired success indicators that you have achieved?

1.

2.

3.

List three desired success indicators that you have *not* achieved?

1.

2.

3.

List three skills and/or areas of knowledge that have contributed to successes you have already achieved. (If you need help, see Appendix A.)

1.

2.

3.

List three things that you *need* to know or do that will lead you to the success you desire.

1.

2.

3.

Chapter 2

IT'S ALL ABOUT PREPARATION AND READINESS

I was twelve years old when I went camping for the first time. As a Girl Scout troop member, I knew that camping in a tent overnight was the ultimate rite of passage into a special bond with my peers. We would prepare our campsite, cook our food over an open fire, and sleep on Mother Nature's precious ground. My heart was bursting with idealized visions of communing in the great outdoors. So I was ready to throw all of my energies into making this experience special.

This camping event involved a number of troops from our area, converging on a large forested area in some pretty tame foothills in New Jersey. Each troop had its own section of woods to build a campsite. We could see the other troops but were not close enough to interact with them. This was a chance for us to practice the camping skills we had been taught at our scout meetings. We lashed limbs together to make a table, cordoned off our camp area with fallen logs, built a rock-lined cooking pit, and put up our tents.

As luck would have it, one of my jobs was to dig the latrine. For some unknown reason, it had never occurred to me that camping did not include access to private bathroom facilities. Nonetheless, the troop leader led me to the desired latrine site, handed me a spade, and instructed me to dig. The task took me about an hour.

During that hour I had plenty of time to think about taking care of my personal bodily functions perched over a hole in the ground. This "bathroom" area was to be equipped with a toilet seat mounted on an orange crate poised over my perfectly dug hole. An assortment of shower curtains were to be strung on the saplings surrounding the "toilet" (someone's idea of privacy) and a roll of TP hung on the branch of a bush.

Everyone in the troop thought our facilities were just terrific—except me. It's true that I had constructed the area according to plan but having to use it didn't appeal to me in the least. As much as I tried to avoid the moment, Nature made her call late in the afternoon. With great trepidation, I ventured beyond the hanging shower curtains. I gingerly perched upon the seat, hoping that no one was nearby. At that moment, a swirling breeze blew through the trees, lifting the curtains high in the air, exposing me to my scout mates and the neighboring campers. It was a moment of pure, preteen mortification. Camping was beginning to lose its charm.

That evening we cooked hot dogs and baked beans over our campfire, followed by s'mores and toasted marshmallows. It was getting colder now that the sun had gone down but we were dressed for it, and the fire was cozy. Finally it was time to retire, so I and my two scout friends headed for our tent. I was tired from all the work and the fresh air, but I was also uneasy about the night. When we got into the tent, I was ready to curl up in my bedroll (not a nice toasty sleeping bag like the others had) and sleep. That was not the plan for my friends.

As I started to change into my pjs, they thought it would be funny to push me outside the tent and close the flap, leaving me half naked in the cold. I tried to be a good sport about it, after all they pulled me back inside in a few seconds, but I still felt embarrassed. I finally got myself together and tucked into bed when the M&M fight started. There were candy pieces flying everywhere. My friends were jumping around the tent, messing up my bedroll, and laughing uproariously. I said to myself, "This isn't at all how I thought it would be." That was to be my first and last camping trip.

This experience taught me another important lesson:

High expectations can be crushed by seemingly minor realities.

Romanticized notions often impede us from looking realistically at our ability to create the outcomes we desire. My perception of camping only included the activities that matched my capabilities and interests. That wasn't enough. Being prepared for the work was one thing: being emotionally ready to rough it was quite another.

Business fitness grounds you in reality and then propels you forward.

Building a successful business life isn't much different than going camping. You need to understand first what you're getting into and whether you're ready to take on the challenge. Whether you're a young scout or a seasoned wilderness adventurer, the requirements are the same: develop and practice the skills you need, assemble essential people and gear, prepare for the risks and challenges of the terrain, and build the physical and mental strength you need to handle success and adversity. Like camping, business is challenging and even fun, but it is not a lark—there is nothing trivial about it. Business mistakes can have serious consequences to you, to others, and to society. When the cold winds of the marketplace blow your shower curtains to the treetops, you don't want to be sitting on your desk chair exposed to the chill if you can help it.

By becoming business fit, you position yourself to:

- Achieve your goals
- Make effective choices
- Take independent action
- Meet increasing performance demands

- Recognize signs of opportunity—avoiding negative forces and seizing positive ones

Achieving business fitness requires the same serious focus and rigorous practice we see demonstrated by great athletes. The formula is really quite simple:

Business Fitness = Preparation + Readiness

Business fitness means that you have what it takes to act successfully at every opportunity. That means that you have the concrete tools you need to make the right things happen and the inner drive to stay the course.

Preparation = Knowledge + Skills + Experience

Preparation builds capability. Believe me, we are rarely fully prepared for the challenges or opportunities that confront us, but we can continue to do much to expand our capabilities to deal with them.

Preparation starts with knowledge. If you're an athlete, success depends on your understanding of the game you're playing—not just today's contest but the game in its broadest sense. In business, like sports, you need to understand what it takes to succeed. You need to know how your competition is performing and what differentiates you from them. As an employee, if you want to get ahead, you need to understand what your options are, what the duties and requirements are of other positions, how to position yourself as a candidate, and what the potential rewards are. Whether you're an entrepreneur or a company employee, you need to understand how business works—politically, economically, and administratively.

Your knowledge of the business environment and your career objectives enable you to prioritize your skill needs and set a path to increase them. Education gives you knowledge and training gives you skills. If you want to be successful, you need both. The list of business skills can be long if you slice the components thinly. But there are some critical ones that, when mastered, set you apart. They are:

- Leadership
- Goal Setting
- Managing Performance
- Planning and Organizing
- Delegating and Controlling
- Communication—oral, written, listening
- Relationship Building
- Influencing, Negotiating, Sales

These skills are the biggies. Once you have developed an ability to use these skills, you will find that you can hold your own in nearly any business situation, particularly when you have the knowledge to go with them.

Experience is what truly sets you apart.

Experience is the icing on the cake. It invariably gives you the edge in any business situation. Knowledge and skills are your performance platform, but legitimate, reality-based experience gives you a perspective and a credibility that is solid. Conference table discussions are replete with ideas about how to increase sales, improve employee morale, reduce costs, and become more competitive. Each participant vies for a chance to present his or her ideas conceptually. The person who presents an idea and backs it up with personal experience is the one who is truly heard and remembered. Nothing beats statements like:

- "I just spent two days in the field talking with our employees."
- "Recently, I had lunch with the union president and his view is this...."
- "I have been working closely for the past three years with our suppliers."
- "I just completed a phone survey with our competitors."
- "My budget reduction initiatives this year have produced these savings."

Experience also demonstrates how your knowledge and skills held up when you were tested under fire. This builds your confidence and captures the confidence of others. By applying your knowledge and skills to real situations, you prove to yourself and others that you are a legitimate player. It confirms that you are prepared to take on current and future challenges.

Readiness = Motivation + Energy + Commitment

Readiness is about your inner makeup, that mysterious conglomerate of ego, self-esteem, courage, drive, belief, and self-confidence. We tend not to think much about whether or not we are personally ready to pursue or accept a work opportunity. If we have any hesitation at all, it is usually about whether or not we think we'll like our new boss, colleagues, or work location. We may also consider how the demands of the new assignment will affect our family and social life. We tend to be lured forward by the promise of more exciting work, increased salary, and a fancier title. So, on the basis of these external factors, we go for it.

Readiness is about our inner selves: that's where the oomph comes from that either makes or breaks our success and satisfaction with the work. If the work provides you with opportunities to learn and grow, it can be energizing. When the demands of assignments include razor-thin deadlines that distress you, you may feel out of sync with the job. On the other hand, if fast-paced decision making gets your juices flowing, you will feel right at home. Understanding your motivational make up means looking squarely at what fueled you in other work situations and then realistically assessing whether the new business opportunity will give you the same juice.

Motivation generates energy. When we're highly motivated to take on a challenge, the energy to put in the hours, take calculated risks, explore new avenues, and overcome obstacles comes easily. When we're unmotivated, it seems we can barely get up from our desks to refill our coffee cups. Energy is an enigma— sometimes it manifests itself in outward activity and other times it fuels mental focus. It is, however, the vehicle that generates momentum. Energy is what it takes to make things happen; it is both depletable and renewable. We all need to understand, nurture, and protect

the personal energy reserves we have, using it construc-
tively and ensuring that we don't squander it on unpro-
ductive and inappropriate activities.

Business provides work that suits various energy
profiles, so we need to be sure we understand what
our profiles are. If you are a studied thinker, interested in creating solutions to complex problems or
innovating new products, you need to take advantage
of opportunities that provide you with an environment compatible with the way you want to work. A bull
pen-type office setting is probably not for you. If you
work best on a team engaged in real-time firefights,
then you will likely prefer an open access work group.
Some people have their energy levels bolstered just by
being with others; some people experience a loss of
energy during extended human interaction. Knowing
what gives you energy and what drains it from you
helps you understand your readiness for any new business opportunity.

If you aren't committed, you aren't ready.

Commitment means that you intend to stick
things out in spite of the difficulties because you believe
in what you're doing. It is your commitment that either
keeps you moving forward or stalls you. If you are committed to your career growth, you will likely take a
chance on a challenging job offer. If you are committed
to making it as an entrepreneur, you will likely take that
risk. If you are committed to doing good for the world,
then you will affiliate yourself with others with the same
desire. Motivation and energy work together to solidify

your commitment to any challenge. Perseverance is made easier when you remain motivated and energized.

Motivation, energy, and commitment are as mutually dependent as knowledge, skills, and experience. When inevitable doubt and disillusionment affect your commitment, motivation will pull you through. When your motivation lags, your commitment will compensate. That's why it is so important to nurture your energy levels—the power source for your continuous forward motion. If you don't feel committed to the business opportunity before you, you are probably not personally ready to accept it.

Achieving business fitness is a matter of balancing preparation and readiness factors. Remember, we are never perfectly prepared or ready for anything. We simply continue to build our fitness. There is always something to work on. So we need to add a little bit to our preparation and readiness tool kit every day. Chapters 4 through 10 detail the essential steps to building your business fitness.

Take Stock of Yourself: Balance Your Seesaw

Preparation and readiness issues make or break new business start-ups, career selections, job changes and promotions, as well as business growth. It is not uncommon for us to look at other people in jobs or careers that interest us and say to ourselves, "I could do that" or "I should be the one doing that job instead of so and so." We are inclined to see the outward performance of others against our assessment of our own skills and abilities. In some cases we may be correct in our assessment; we may very well be better for that job, but we also may not be seeing the entire picture. Here's what can happen when a work-life decision is made when you are prepared but not ready to make a move.

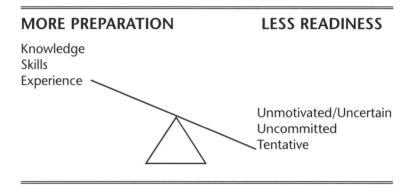

MORE PREPARATION   **LESS READINESS**

Knowledge
Skills
Experience

Unmotivated/Uncertain
Uncommitted
Tentative

Roberta is a technical specialist who aspires to become a first line supervisor—a positive step in her career growth. Roberta recognized that in order to move from an individual contributor position to a supervisory one, she needed to develop new skills. So for the past three years, she attended company-offered training courses on planning and organizing, delegating and controlling, communications, and performance management. She knew that her technical knowledge was the best in the department because of the feedback from her boss and her peers. All she needed to do now was to wait for a supervisory opening.

When her boss resigned, Roberta was perfectly positioned to take the job based on her knowledge and skills. Although she hadn't had any real supervisory experience, she had covered for her boss many times when he was out of the office. So Roberta was a lock for the job, and when her promotion came through, she was elated. In her mind, her preparation had truly paid off. Unfortunately, preparation is not always enough.

Roberta had high expectations when she took the reins as supervisor for her old work unit. She had been friends with two of the technical specialists and the administrative person who were now reporting to her and they fully understood their work. It didn't take long before she hired a new college grad to backfill her old position. That's when the problems began.

A couple of her former peers didn't support her new hire and resented the plum assignments that Roberta gave him. Roberta soon realized that one of her former co-workers was not as productive and careful as she needed to be—a situation that needed to be corrected. Her new boss, the department manager, demanded status reports and budget accountabilities that were foreign to her. She became unnerved by her boss and avoided contact with him. She was hurt by the way her old work mates criticized her so she avoided them too. Little by little she started doing some of her old work since it made her feel more productive and safe. This was the beginning of the end of Roberta's career as a supervisor.

This was a terrible waste for Roberta and her company. She thought she was prepared for her new job but soon learned that her understanding of her supervisory role was lacking. The work demands of her boss were things she didn't know how to do. Because she was not committed to overcoming the interpersonal challenges of her new assignment, she lost her zeal, her optimism, and her self-confidence as well as her motivation. Unfortunately, too many business leaders fail to notice when an employee is struggling, or if they do notice, they fail to help. All too often, there is a prevailing sink-or-swim attitude in the workplace, no matter what the position. If Roberta had been prepared for the unseen skill requirements of supervision and had been committed to conquering the challenges of supervision, her success in that position would have been far more likely.

There are also success risks when we are ready but not prepared for opportunities that present themselves. This applies when we are so caught up in optimistic business expectations that we ignore the realities. Here's what it looks like to be more ready than prepared to take an important step:

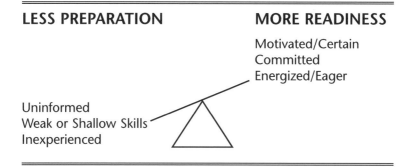

LESS PREPARATION   **MORE READINESS**

Motivated/Certain
Committed
Energized/Eager

Uninformed
Weak or Shallow Skills
Inexperienced

One of the reasons that many small businesses fail is that budding entrepreneurs have more enthusiasm for their new enterprises than they do applied capabilities. Let's take Charlie for example.

Charlie was a perennial kid at heart and always wanted to have his own business selling unique toys for small children. He'd spent seemingly hundreds of hours in large toy store chains shopping for his children and then his grandchildren. So when he was downsized from his production line job, he thought this was the time to start his own business.

Over the years, he had found and stayed in contact with a number of cottage industry toy makers—people he'd met at craft and specialty shows. Six of these craftspeople were willing to consign their products to Charlie who would market them when he was ready to launch his business. Charlie was psyched to get started.

He began by renting a small storefront in his suburban town, hanging out a sign, building displays, and printing business cards. His consignors sent him a modest supply of their toys. Charlie had a few antique toys that he was willing to part with so he added them to the inventory. He told his friends, announced his new business at his church, ran a small ad in his local paper, and opened for business. On the first weekend, his friends and family came and congratulated him on his new venture. They bought a couple of toys in support. After that, there was very little traffic in his store. He'd sit there for hours each day and see a couple of stragglers who came out of curiosity. Naturally, Charlie became very discouraged and struggled to figure out what had gone wrong. He had toys that were well made and unique—he knew that from all of his research. They were fairly priced for their quality. But his business was failing.

Charlie knew a lot about toys but not very much about running a business, particularly about business planning and marketing. His lack of understanding of what consumers in his area wanted and how to promote the uniqueness of his business created neither buzz nor traffic. His inventory was too thin and his location selection not prominent. He failed to recognize that a small business requires the same professional capabilities as a large one—it's all a matter of degree. Charlie's enthusiasm to make an entrepreneurial dream come true blinded him to the realities and disciplines of running a successful business.

Achieving business fitness and the work life success that goes with it requires a balance between preparation and readiness.

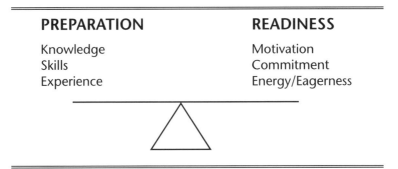

PREPARATION   **READINESS**

Knowledge   Motivation
Skills   Commitment
Experience   Energy/Eagerness

We are never completely prepared or completely ready when a good business or career opportunity presents itself. But if we understand our success indicators and our options for obtaining them, we always have a sense of the work we need to do to enhance our capabilities— our skills, knowledge, and experiences—and build our readiness levels.

Practice—Practice—Practice

Successful athletes work on their physical conditioning every day and challenge their mental toughness by competing regularly in pickup games and regular season contests, always looking toward the play-offs. They practice game fundamentals over and over and over again. They practice them alone, they practice them with personal coaches, and they practice them with their teammates. The dread of all athletes is injury. Why is that? Because they can't practice and they can't play, which means they lose their edge and their fitness. Rehabilitating an injury is challenging but so is getting an athlete's strength, agility, eye, and timing back. The only way to do that is by practice. The more they practice, the better they get.

Just like athletes, we, as businesspeople, need to stay business fit by practicing our skills every day and challenging our mettle in the day-to-day transactions of the workplace and marketplace. There are skills that we can practice alone like written communication and planning; there are skills that we can practice with our professional coaches or supervisors like presentation skills and problem-solving. Some skills we can practice with others like leading, negotiating, relationship building, and delegation.

Our practice is at times alone in our offices and at other times in live action. It includes understanding required skills, using them, reviewing the results in retrospect (like screening post-game films), and practicing some more, building our confidence along the way. For those of us in business, the play-offs are those precious business or career opportunities that present themselves fleetingly. We need to be prepared and ready to seize those moments. The more we practice, the sharper and quicker we get.

The Cast: How Some Have Ridden the Seesaw

No success or performance model is ever as neat and clean as it looks. That goes for my seesaw model for preparation and readiness. But models give us a way to visualize our own behavior, our personal plans of action, and the impacts of our choices. As a tool, a model increases clarity about our behavior and enhances our ability to choose next steps. The cast of characters you met in Chapter 1 has experienced differing degrees of preparation and readiness in their pursuit of business success. Here is a brief look at the way the model applied to a couple of these people.

A Quick Rise and a Hard Fall

Cliff Black thought he was perfectly well prepared to move from a plant general manager to district vice president. After all, he was responsible for the management and production of a major company facility that included a staff of white and blue collar workers, substantial production requirements, and complex equipment. He knew exactly how the business operated on all levels. He was considered a good leader based on the loyalty of his employees and a good manager because of the performance of his plant. He was confident that he had all the preparation he needed to move on, and so did the executive who was promoting him.

Cliff loved his plant work and *his* people. He was committed to them and their plant and everyone knew it. He came to work each day motivated and energized to maintain a pristine facility and a reliable source of product. But those conditions were gone when he became district VP. Cliff never assessed the significance of the status and relationships he was giving up to take his new job. So he went to captain a new ship without his old, loyal shipmates.

What hurt Cliff's ability to redirect his skills and knowledge was an inherent weakness in his readiness to take on this new role. All Cliff needed was some time to learn the ropes and some support from trusted people around him. When he didn't get either, his confidence steadily eroded.

Cliff's connection to the district employees and community were not as strong as they had been at the plant. He didn't know anyone there and they didn't know him. He was a foreigner of sorts and was made to feel that way. When he failed to get strong support from his new staff, his commitment and motivation to excel started to decline. His new challenges required a tolerance for ambiguity that Cliff lacked. All of this sapped his energy and in the end caused his fall.

There are many in Cliff's situation who continue to hang on—dangling from a precarious business post like a corporate Garfield.

Sometimes a Hard Ride Is a Good Ride

Doug Hart is a courageous guy—seemingly fearless in business. That's what makes him so exciting to know. Remember how he started out as a business major and became a specialist in cardiac catheter technology, moving from hospital work to sales. When Doug launched his career in the highly competitive medical product sales field, he knew that he would have to endure rookie status for a good long while. He also knew that he had no big-time sales experience and few firing line successes closing deals and beating the competition. Doug is a guy who recognizes his talents and understands how to adapt them to new situations. He has a sharp eye for the politics of the marketplace, particularly an ability to read the agenda of those around him.

Although Doug was not fully prepared for the demands of medical product sales, he was astute enough to sense that it was going to be difficult, full of surprises (many of them unpleasant), and a test of his nerve. He took on this industry as a personal challenge. He was committed to find success, no matter how hard he had to work. So he went for it.

One thing Doug wasn't short on was energy. He is a classic type-A personality and it shows up in his personal and work life. He thrives on the excitement of business—turning prospects into customers, an opportunity into a done deal, and a new product into a winner.

Doug's energy level was the well from which he drew when things were rough in the sales biz. When he started with his first medical products firm, he was low man. He knew if he didn't produce in short order, he would be out. He struggled to understand how the big hitters were making and exceeding their quotas. He studied what they did; he tried new angles of his own. Some worked and some didn't. Every now and then, he'd make a good sale and then he'd go for a long while, following what seemed to be an endless trail of rejections or delays from client prospects.

Doug had a knack for analyzing his missteps and correcting them. He'd find a way to see something positive in every move—knowing that he had to see progress to sustain his motivation. When things got dark, he returned to his commitment to find success in this industry. He refilled his energy tank by finding ways to build client relationships through recreational outings—golf, sporting events, dinners. He worked through the hard times by always focusing on the results he was seeking. And that's exactly what he got in the end—the success he wanted.

In Doug's case he knew he was ready for a challenge although he didn't fully know how demanding it would be. Even though he didn't initially have the sales preparation that was essential for success, he had the energy and commitment to build his capabilities along the way. Commitment and confidence are a powerful combination; that's why, in this case, Doug was able to ride the rough water and end up on top.

In a Nutshell

Preparation and readiness don't always come from predictable places. We each command a unique set of knowledge, skills, and experiences regardless of where we are on our career path. We need to build on that foundation relentlessly. We each have a core of desire that is our source of motivation, commitment, and energy. You build preparation and readiness a little every day. As you build one you can enhance the other—expanding your overall business fitness.

You increase your opportunities for success by creating momentum through actions that are a product of your preparation and readiness. Momentum takes you where you want to go—it is the ride that you create for yourself. You build it and you control it by what you do in private and what you demonstrate in public.

YOUR PREPARATION AND READINESS INVENTORY

Your business fitness is the result of your preparation and readiness to move forward. You increase your likelihood for success by assessing your knowledge, skills, and experience plus your motivation, commitment, and energy. The more balance you have between preparation and readiness, the better positioned you are to take that next step.

Describe briefly the next career or business move you would like to make.

List the knowledge, skills, and experiences required for that move? Put an "X" beside the ones that you currently possess. Circle the ones that you need to develop.
(If you need help, see Appendix A.)

Knowledge	Skills	Experience
1.	1.	1.
2.	2.	2.
3.	3.	3.
4.	4.	4.
5.	5.	5.

List the motivation, commitment, and energy that are required? Write a phrase that describes how you will meet those requirements.

Motivation	Commitment	Energy
1.	1.	1.
2.	2.	2.
3.	3.	3.
4.	4.	4.
5.	5.	5.

What is your timetable for building your preparation and readiness for this next opportunity?

Chapter 3

THE POWER OF MOMENTUM: PRIVATE MOVES AND PUBLIC MOVES

When I was a senior in high school, I convinced my parents to let me have a big party toward the end of football season. It was to be an open house for the team and the cheerleaders.

The air was cold and the stars were spectacular on that Saturday evening in October. There were sodas and hot dogs and all sorts of things to nibble on. The party was outside on our patio where my friends could hang out and even shoot some hoops. Everyone was in great spirits, reminiscing about the year, enjoying some romantic snuggling, and sharing funny stories. It was just the kind of party I had imagined—a warm gathering of friends who had shared a special part of their youth together. All was going perfectly.

There were about sixty kids gathered so the food was going fast. I went into the kitchen for more snacks and, to my surprise, a teenage boy was sitting there nursing a badly sprained ankle. The problem was that I had no idea who this kid was or the other two guys with him. Little by little there emerged a growing number of outsiders arriving at the party—the number of kids had grown to 100. These teens were from other towns a distance away—this was not a good thing. I let my parents know what was happening and they remained a lot calmer than I did.

About an hour later, one of my friends reported that her purse was gone and then another and another. My parents called the police who arrived quickly and cordoned off our street. They interviewed the girls with stolen purses but there really wasn't much the police could do. The party was halted, everyone was quietly ushered off, and I was left very sad.

With a heavy heart, I learned this:

Circumstances can change in an instant and quickly build a powerful head of steam.

The good news is that the girls got their purses back. They were found tossed in a vacant lot, the wallets significantly lighter. My parents never bemoaned the party or my good intentions. They dealt with the turn of events quickly and efficiently, identifying problems and making decisions without hesitation. We all concluded that characterizing the event as an open house was not a good idea—an important marketing lesson. I learned that even though the party was going well—just as I had planned—that didn't mean conditions couldn't change. Once outside factors intruded, the problems escalated. I also learned that when a situation starts taking a downward spiral, quick mitigating action can minimize the damage.

**Business fitness increases your ability
to manage momentum.**

Business events showcase the decisions you make and the actions you take. Many business initiatives start out well, take a downward turn, and then recover; sometimes they even start out poorly and finish well. The point is if you are clear about where you're headed, align your actions with your goals, and make effective decisions in the face of tough conditions, you increase your odds of successfully controlling the momentum, sustaining the positive and defusing the negative.

**Every new action builds on the last—
that's how you create momentum.**

Momentum is about movement. You need to act repeatedly and consistently to build it. Success is a by-product of effectively managed momentum. Some of your actions will create the outcomes you want and others will not. As stupid as we may feel when we have made a mess of things, the information we get from our missteps is invaluable. The key is to keep moving forward, steadily removing obstacles, realigning relationships, and following new opportunities. When you get on a roll, enjoy the ride—but don't spend too much time coasting. If you do, you'll eventually slow to a stop.

When you find yourself on that inevitable "everything seems to be going wrong" cycle, keep pedaling even when you would rather stop and get off your bike. At times it may be prudent to pedal slowly to get your bearings and decide on a better course. Sometimes, it may be smart to accelerate initiatives to correct errors, circumvent problems, or pursue new resources. The key is not to let disappointments and stressful conditions affect your momentum. What you learn during a backslide will likely become the information you need to propel you forward later at a greater rate. Your success is measured both by the concrete outcomes you achieve and by the knowledge, skills, and experience that increase your storehouse of unique capabilities. Remember this:

**Trial and error is a good thing.
It's one way you figure things out.**

Each time you survive a period of trial you are in a position to inventory your lessons learned. I learned from my party that positive momentum quickly succumbed to negative momentum when the first purse was stolen. Everything after that was a downward spiral.

It was the corrective momentum created by my parents' quick actions to address the problem—calling the police and ending the party—that ended the negative momentum and returned the calm. These lessons learned served me well and taught me this:

A small step forward takes you farther than no step at all—particularly when you follow it with another.

Managing business and career momentum is a lot like controlling the speed of your car. Sometimes you need to step on the gas; other times you can glide along at the speed limit and enjoy the sights. You may periodically need to stop completely when traffic is backed up. The point is that when you're driving somewhere you're committed to reaching a destination. So when you need to adjust the momentum of your vehicle to get there safely, you do it almost without thinking. When there are traffic problems or detours, it is rare that you would give up on your trip; instead you simply adjust your speed.

Momentum motivates you to stay focused on your destination—your success indicators—and keep moving forward at the best pace you can muster. You empower yourself when you realize that you are in a position to manage that momentum. You may not be able to control the circumstances around you, but you can manage the steps you take that keep you on track.

The benefits of momentum are as dramatic as the lack of it. Here's what it can look like when you

confront the state of your business or career momentum head-on:

POSITIVE OR FORWARD MOMENTUM	NEGATIVE OR BACKWARD MOMENTUM	NO MOMENTUM
Progress each day	Feelings of chaos	Boredom
Optimism	Pessimism	Pessimism
Exponential growth	Loss of ground	No progress
Results attainment	Lack of success	Distraction
Increasing confidence	Lack of confidence	Lack of confidence
Energy and eagerness	Stress and frustration	Malaise
Increased innovation	Confusion and helplessness	Increasing procrastination

The Cast of Characters:
He Who Drives Controls the Ride

The challenge of managing momentum is sens-
ing it in the first place. Sometimes we get so caught up
in our daily tasks and the buzz of the workplace that we
fail to size up the activities that are swirling around us.
Sometimes we simply don't want to think about where
all of this activity may lead because then we might have
to change what we are doing. When the momentum of
events appears to be moving in a desirable direction,
we're happy to ride the crest of the wave. But when
activities take a negative turn and develop a downward
spiral, we often want to look the other way.

Here are the stories of two of our cast members
who experienced the impacts of momentum, both positive and negative. I've included my own story as well.

When You're in a Ditch, Call a Tow Truck

When Dr. Barker's office manager, Jeanette, quit, he had to come to grips with operational and morale issues that had been festering in his practice for a long time. This is what was going on:

- Personnel policy implementation was inconsistent
- The Office Manager was overextended
- Scheduling of hours was rigid and arbitrary
- There was no formal skills training
- Communication was haphazard and ineffective

These issues had emerged slowly and had now reached a peak. As each issue built on the other, the declining morale escalated. This is how these unaddressed issues impacted employees:

- Growing pessimism about their future at the practice
- Feelings of helplessness and professional stagnation
- Open resistance to some policies
- Frustration with their inability to influence decisions
- A belief that they were being unfairly treated
- Disillusionment with the leadership

These perceptions became high-octane fuel for negative momentum.

As staff members shared their complaints with each other, rolling them together to form a monolith of negative energy, the unwanted momentum gained a

solid foothold in the practice. It was time to take stock
and reverse the negative momentum. Here's what Dr.
Barker did:

- Revised personnel policies
- Redesigned scheduling procedures
- Provided paid training opportunities
- Realigned the Officer Manager's work
- Created career growth opportunities

By recognizing the value of satisfied and engaged
employees to his practice, Dr. Barker made changes
that turned negative, debilitating momentum into positive, restorative momentum. His actions:

- Restored employee confidence in the leadership
- Created optimism about the long-term effects
  of improvements
- Restored employee energy and eagerness to
  perform well
- Improved individual and practice performance results overall

Because Dr. Barker acted quickly to bring
Jeanette back to the practice and got consultant help,
he quite literally stopped the bleeding in his practice.
His actions gave employees a voice, shutting down the
escalation of negative momentum, and creating a new
energy that built positive momentum. Not only did
these changes improve morale, they improved practice
profitability as well. He maintained that forward
momentum until he sold the practice after a forty-year

run—not a bad payback for his willingness to tackle tough issues and see them through to resolution.

Beware of Cruise Control

When Hal Dodger took a position at corporate headquarters, he had high hopes that his career would blossom. What Hal didn't know was that this new assignment was an effort by the company to see whether he could be more successful in a staff position than he was in the field. There were serious questions about his capabilities, although they had not been effectively communicated to him. So Hal used the same approaches in his new job that he did in his old.

The culture of the corporate office was foreign to Hal, as were the performance standards, requirements, and pressures. He floundered at his work and frustrated his boss. When Hal was reassigned, he again thought this move was part of his development. It was evident pretty quickly that he was not able to adapt to this new internal consultant role either. He missed deadlines. He botched up meetings and the processes that defined his work.

Hal never quite understood how all of these issues overtook him. He was neither the architect of positive nor negative momentum because he just did what he had always done job after job. Hal came to work on cruise control—operating at the same speed on the same open highway day after day. He never had any sense of variation, new direction or obstacles. He just stared straight-ahead, mesmerized by that constant speed.

This is what happened to Hal because he lacked a sense of his career momentum, forward or backward, positive or negative:

- He made little progress with his internal clients
- He was unable to complete projects because he couldn't stay focused
- He missed deadlines because he was distracted and disorganized
- He lost confidence in his abilities, so he tried to off-load tasks to others
- He alienated his peers who often had to cover for him

Without momentum, we wither. Momentum is essential to growth, progress, optimism, and success. As troubling as negative momentum can be, it is still movement. We can use our creative instincts, innovative problem-solving skills, and passion for our work to convert negative momentum into the positive. It is generally more difficult to overcome inertia—the absence of momentum—because there is nothing that pushes us forward.

Hal Dodger lost his job because of his inability to recognize and then do something about his decline. He lacked necessary skills and business savvy, but he could have corrected that if he had been willing to make significant changes. Instead, he let the paralysis of denial and lost momentum take control of his work life.

Accelerate Aggressively When You Must

Momentum is contagious. I learned this on two levels during my first year working for a large service corporation.

After a decade-long career teaching high school, I was fortunate to land a job as an educational programs coordinator for a Fortune 500 company. Corporate life felt like the perfect place for me. I was truly in my element—developing a strategy to develop unbiased consumer education materials. But building this strategy and the accompanying tactical plan was a big job, requiring the involvement of a host of high level leaders, departments, community organizations, and my project team. Little by little, the plan came together until it was ready to be presented to the CEO and his executive council.

This was my big moment. I had built the plan and knew the details inside and out. Since I'd spent so much time on my feet in front of student groups, I felt reasonably comfortable about presenting the material although, I must admit, knowing this was to be a conference room full of the corporate brass was a bit daunting. The upside was that since I was clearly a rookie in the company with only twelve months on the job, I didn't fully comprehend the fiscal and political implications of what I was about to propose. I certainly didn't know what effect, if any, it might have on my career. I was just very excited to have the chance to offer something of educational value to our consumers.

The presentation went off without a hitch. It was the question and answer period that became the next hurdle. The CEO asked for clarification of some points, the COO offered a few observations, and then the CFO asked a key question.

"The budget and resource commitments for this effort seem reasonable, Dawn," he said. "What I need to know is when will Phase I of the initiative be complete. We don't want this to become a protracted effort."

Can you believe it? I'd never thought about exactly when I would wrap up Phase I. My brain was racing and I knew intuitively that if I didn't answer this question definitively, the positive momentum I'd achieved to that moment would be dampened.

Without a moment's hesitation, I said, "Phase I will be completed in six months, and I will provide a report to this group on its effectiveness two weeks thereafter."

"That sounds fine," the CFO answered and the program was approved.

Now I'd done it. I had committed to a pace of activity that I had no idea I could achieve, and I'd staked my fledgling reputation on my ability to achieve it. As you can imagine, I had no intention of not completing that project in that six months if it meant that I had to work every waking moment to do it. But that seemingly reckless declaration came to underscore the power of momentum.

Once everyone involved in this project knew where the end zone was, every decision was made and weighed with an eye toward it. The deadline motivated all of us because we wanted to prove that we could deliver. The more progress we made, the more momentum we generated to propel us toward the next requirement. The process created energy and excitement, a feeling of powerfulness and confidence, and a camaraderie that sustained us through the stressful times and fueled our joy during the successes.

Momentum needs to start with a goal or intention. Then it needs to be perpetuated each day by action. Developing a reputation in business for being someone who knows how to get things done can be built by skillfully creating and maintaining momentum that delivers valued results.

Making Your Move

Business fitness evolves from the actions you take. The more you build momentum to increase your preparation and readiness to move forward, the more you create the opportunities and results you are seeking.

For successful athletes there are basically two categories of moves. First is the steady, consistent kind—the moves that are the bread and butter of the game. A golfer keeps making par. A tennis player relentlessly returns the opponent's ground strokes waiting for an error. The defensive line shuts down the offense's running game. These moves are the backbone of the contest. There is nothing particularly spectacular about them individually, yet they are the foundation for winning. The daily training regimen of athletes centers on building and honing individual and team play, positioning them to outperform their opponents move by move.

Secondly, successful athletes know that, in order to win, they must be ready to make an outstanding move—a move that sets them a part, showcasing their exceptional talent and courage—at just the right time. These are the clutch moves; the game-winning moves. The golfer holes a treacherous putt on the 18th green to win the championship. The tennis player fires a second-serve ace at match point. The defensive line creates a quarterback sack on the twelve-yard-line. Athletes live for these moments. When interviewed about them, they often talk about how they had dreamt about those moments from the time they were ten years old. Their years of hard work and training prepare them for those special moments when they are called upon to show what they can really do.

Although it may not appear to be that glamorous, success in business relies on the right moves at the right time by people who are as business fit as the athlete is game fit. Business fitness is built on two kinds of moves: private moves and public moves.

Private Moves

Private moves are the actions you take quietly on your own and without fanfare. They center on building the foundation you need to take advantage of opportunity. They build the strength that you can draw on without thinking when you need to act—as an athlete draws on muscle memory and competitive instinct. Private moves build platforms—the framework, relationships, knowledge base, and skills—that you need to achieve the success you want, *your* way and on your terms. These private moves are your power base, the launching pad for your success today and throughout your future.

Private moves are simple to express but require dedication and consistent application to make them work for you. These moves become a state of being, a reliable set of conditions. The broader and more ingrained they are, the more confident you will be when you draw on them.

There are four private moves:
- Stay Well
- Stay Focused

- Stay Current
- Stay Connected

Each one grounds you. In order to "stay" grounded in these four moves, you need to stay committed to building them a little every day. The more you recognize how the private moves contribute to your success, the more momentum you will build to keep working on them.

Unlike a workout regimen, you enhance your private moves during the daily routine of your work life—recognizing opportunities, working on goals, developing relationships, building knowledge and skills, and deepening your resolve to succeed. As you will learn in Part II, each private move becomes a tool to position you to increase your options in the marketplace.

Public Moves

Public moves are those actions that you take in full view of others, showcasing your capabilities and your commitments. For athletes, public moves take place on game day. This is when they demonstrate their skills, game savvy, and competitive toughness to both their fans and their detractors. Your public moves are the actions that define you. They fill a need, make a difference, ease concerns, redirect attention, and create new opportunities.

Public moves are risks, albeit of varying degrees, and risks are how we test ourselves, build confidence, achieve important results, and learn essential lessons. Very few of our public moves are like the Super Bowl, Wimbledon, or the Masters. Each one, however, has its significance to your workplace environment because it enhances or reduces your momentum.

The three public moves are overt actions:

- Attract a Following
- Take the Lead
- Implement New Ideas

On the surface these moves don't seem too daunting, and they aren't when your private moves give you a strong foundation to take those actions. Every public move has roots in the private moves.

Each one of us has a natural talent for some of these moves and a discomfort with others. Part III will explain each of the public moves in detail. But it is important to understand this:

Each public move becomes part of your workplace history for good or ill.

This means that you need to be smart and strategic about your public moves. It does not mean to be afraid and tentative. Game day comes around whether or not the athlete is fully prepared or completely healthy. Seasoned athletes know how to adjust their games to each situation, not getting too cute or overly aggressive in their play, minimizing error or injury in games that do not impact their season. These athletes protect themselves on multiple levels by playing smart when in the public eye. They protect their reputations by ensuring the best possible performance on game day. They protect their bodies by making good decisions while competing aggressively. They understand the consequences of their performance in the eyes of the fans, the media, and their franchise. They also recognize the link between their ongoing play and their future contract value.

The business environment is your field of play. The eyes are on you when you perform, and each set of eyes assesses you and your contribution to the organization. Your peers and your supervisors *see* what you do. The hierarchy *hears* about what you do. Those in support positions (administrative and facilities personnel) *talk about* what you do. And in some cases, your customers, vendors, and the community do a bit of each.

The important thing to remember is this:

You control the things you do— both your private and public moves.

Business fitness provides you with a framework to maximize your preparation and readiness to step out into the public eye on secure footing, so you can create and take advantage of opportunities that will move your business life forward. It is all in your hands.

In a Nutshell

Momentum requires a series of actions that build on one another. If you can't, don't, or won't take repeated, progressive actions, you will not generate the momentum you need to propel you forward over time. Lots of people take steps that they believe will lead them to success, but they never seem to get very far. All momentum, however, is not linear which means the moves you make need to be flexible.

Business fitness enables you to understand the kind of success you really want and the paths to achieving it. The power to succeed your way comes from choosing to build your own business fitness day by day from now on. The more conscientious your effort, the greater your progress, and the more momentum you create. On top of that you will also have fun making the right things happen on your terms.

YOUR MOMENTUM INVENTORY

Awareness of momentum in the events around you is your first step to understanding how to create and manage it to help you move forward. The better you are at identifying the factors that contribute to momentum, the more able you will be to build positive momentum and keep it working in your favor.

Situation 1: Describe one outcome in your business or personal life that was successfully completed in less than three months.

List the Progression of Events	Month/Year	Who Helped

Situation 2: Select one initiative in your business or personal life that died on the vine.

List the Progression of Events	Month/Year	Who Helped

Momentum Analysis: For each initiative described above, list the positive momentum factors and the momentum killers in the chart below.

Positive Momentum Factors	Momentum Killers
Situation 1:	Situation 1:
Situation 2:	Situation 2:

Lessons Learned: In each situation above, what could you have done differently to manage your momentum better?

PART TWO

PRIVATE MOVES

Chapter 4

STAY WELL

The better you feel, the better you will perform

Don't do it! Please don't skip this chapter. I know you're tired of all the nagging about losing weight, exercising, and giving up unhealthy habits. Those messages are everywhere, and they can get on my nerves too.

I'm not here to lecture you on those things. There are lots of experts out there who can do a better job of that than I can. But you need to understand the relationship between being well and being successful. That's the first step in becoming business fit.

**When you don't feel well,
you don't perform at the top of your game.**

Your ability to become and remain business fit rides on your physical health and your state of mind. Your wellness is the fuel that propels you forward. It's what makes you believe that you can achieve the success you want. It's your source of energy, optimism, courage, and strength. Think about the last time you were sick and how effective you were confronting a co-worker or customer about a problem or how thorough you were in developing a proposal for a new product. Think about the last time you were upset or saddened about something in your life. In that emotional state, how eager were you to help a peer on a rush job? What kind of energy did you bring to a work group meeting to develop a new strategy?

Staying well is what you do to manage how you feel, ensuring that you are always in the best physical and mental condition to showcase your capabilities and take advantage of opportunities. Staying well is a private move that helps you build a reliable store-house of energy and optimism—it's your power source for increasing preparation and readiness to move forward.

Here's the process for staying well:

- Protect yourself as much as possible from ill-ness, injury, and negative self-talk
- Take care of yourself when you become ill or hurt and take overt steps to counteract nega-tive thinking

- Manage chronic physical and mental wellness
  issues relentlessly

Protecting yourself means just that—first knowing what
your health risks are and then taking action to anticipate and avoid them. This is everything from washing
your hands to losing weight to wearing your seat belt.
Taking care of yourself is another way of saying, don't
wait until you can barely get out of bed before you get
medical care. It also means recognizing that a single
day in bed, sleeping and caring for your symptoms, will
likely increase the speed of your recovery. To minimize
the negative impacts of chronic health issues, you need
to understand fully what is required to achieve and sustain a reasonably predictable level of wellness and then
to take those steps religiously.

   Staying well mentally and emotionally is also a
key to your success. Where there are serious mental and
emotional issues, professional medical care is essential.
However, a great many of us suffer from something that
is well within our control—that's negative self-talk. To
stay well emotionally and ensure a forward path to business fitness, we all need to avoid negative feedback that
we direct at ourselves.

   We hurt ourselves when we say how stupid we are
to ever think we would be considered for a promotion.
We weaken ourselves when we say, "I can't take on that
assignment. I don't know enough. I'm not smart
enough. No one will ever listen to me." It happens
when we tell ourselves that we'll never be anything but
a secretary, a salesman, a technician, or a field worker.
It's when you say, "I can never get a job like that because

I don't have an MBA or enough experience. I've only worked in customer service, so no one would consider me for a job in marketing."

Negative self-talk creates attitudinal "un-wellness." Over time it sickens the spirit and paralyzes your ability to move forward. It's equally or more debilitating to your success than nearly any physical affliction. Fortunately, negative self-talk is quite easy to correct and you control the "cure."

Think about this. Your mind will answer any question you ask it. So if you ask yourself, "Why don't I ever get promoted?" Your mind will answer, "Because you don't have the right credentials, you're stuck in a job that doesn't give you any visibility, and your supervisor doesn't put in a good word for you." There you have it. Now you know.

The fact is that your mind doesn't always know the truth and neither do you. But if you ask yourself a different question, your mind will likely give you a more positive and useful answer. This time you ask, "What can I do to make myself a more attractive candidate for a promotion." Now your mind will answer, "Talk to your supervisor about your interest in a new position and what you could be doing to increase your knowledge and experiences so you will at least be considered. Find out from the human resources department what the skill sets are for positions you're interested in. Take some skill development courses. Talk to the hiring managers and ask them what you could do to make yourself a more desirable candidate."

By asking a solutions-oriented question, you end up with a set of actions that will move you toward the success you want. These answers help you create momentum toward your goals. They focus you on the means to the end, not just the end itself. This new momentum may ultimately lead you to an even better outcome than you first anticipated. You never know unless you get in gear.

When it comes to negative feedback, we are often our own worst enemies. The more we try to achieve perfection, the harder we are on ourselves. This cripples our readiness to move forward. Negative self-talk that tears you down creates a sickened spirit. The greater the dose the more debilitating it is. Look around you. Are the people that you consider successful negative about their performance? Are the athletes you hear interviewed after a losing game negative about themselves? Or do they see the upside of their loss? Instead of being negative, aren't they saying how much they learned about the strong and weak points of their game preparation and strategy? Aren't they talking about how they are going to increase their efforts to play better? Aren't they reinforcing how much talent and capability they know they have, saying that they are great players who simply had a bad game?

You rarely hear standout athletes saying that they stink and that their poor play is just another indication of what losers they are. Instead, they take a lessons-learned approach to adversity, reexamine their regimen, recast their strategy, and intensify their commitment to success. Why don't we do more of that at *our* jobs? Why do so many of us punish ourselves, complain, gripe, blame, and second-guess? It's the sickness of negativity.

In the early 1980s, my boss sent me to a seminar for women in management, a daylong program focusing

on unique issues women leaders faced in corporate settings. I remember one very important message from
the seminar leader. She told us that in business and in
life *stay away from negative people.* This is a very powerful statement, and I have followed it since then.
Negative people hold you back. They give you all the
reasons why you can't or shouldn't, why that won't
work, why this person is not good enough, and how all
the evils of the world will befall you if you take that step.

The tough thing about avoiding negative people
is that sometimes they are people you love—even your
immediate family and longtime friends. Sometimes
they are also your boss, your peers, or your employees—
people you need to work with every day. When that's
the case, you need to take careful steps to demonstrate
to them how a positive and constructive perspective creates opportunities for everyone's benefit—how it creates a healthier work environment. If the negative people around you become a weight that you can't afford
to bear, then you need to de-couple yourself from them,
even if that means minimizing contact, avoiding conversation on certain topics, or finding another place to
work. I know this isn't easy, but in the long run your success depends upon it.

**It's not always whether you're healthy that matters,
but whether you seem healthy.
If you actually are healthy, that's a bonus.**

Clearly, everyone gets sick at one time or another,
some more than others. We never know if we'll be the
ones with temporary or long-term health setbacks at

some time in our lives. We also experience traumatic, personal events that can drag us down—divorce, problems with children, financial issues, and disappointments of all kinds. Just because these situations can and perhaps already have happened to you, it doesn't mean that you should allow them to define you, particularly at work.

The organizations that employ us or the businesses that we own are entities of someone's creation. Company leaders and owners define the business and establish the rules of operation. Employees do the work that enables the business to be successful and in return we expect to find success ourselves. Just as the business relies on positive public and customer perceptions for success, our ability to succeed within that business relies on perceptions too. We need our leaders and peers to regard us as reliable, dependable, committed, and capable. That's how we attract opportunity. The most critical and most obvious perception we create is our *vitality*, and vitality is a function of our wellness.

We all have times when we don't feel up to par, that's a given. Your success opportunities are compromised when you have more than the occasional bout with sickness, injury, or emotional turmoil. There are degrees of "un-wellness"—everything from the common cold to pneumonia. So "un-wellness" issues are either occasional, seasonal, or chronic. The success impacts of "un-wellness" often have more to do with timing that they do with frequency.

Let's say that you have a terrible cold. You are running a low-grade fever accompanied by a sinus headache, congestion, and a dry cough. We've all shared your discomfort and have gotten ourselves to work regardless. Because you feel so bad, you plan to use the day to respond to e-mails, complete some administrative work, and do some planning—things that don't require any complex thinking or interactions with others.

On this day, though, your boss calls and asks you to meet with him in an hour to discuss a special assignment that will require you to build and implement an action plan to increase product production to meet immediate customer demand. Before the meeting he wants you to think about how you might approach this initiative since the plan needs to be finalized by the end of the week.

Needless to say, you're thinking that this is not the time to feel this sick. You'd been waiting for a chance to take the lead on an important effort and here it is on the one day you feel terrible. Now, in one hour, you need to come up with a credible approach to this challenge when your head is pounding.

You bring your ideas to the meeting and your boss finds them acceptable, but your ability to display energy and enthusiasm is stifled by your struggle to breathe. The idea of completing this important plan by the end of the week makes your palms sweat. Sadly, because you aren't well, the excitement of this important moment is gone. Your boss, although knowing you are ill, is concerned that you may not be able to do your best job because of it. So, neither of you leaves the meeting with high optimism.

We can paint this scenario in lots of ways. Whether it's your big chance to lead a team, interview for a new position, meet new colleagues or customers, make a speech, or deliver a proposal, if you don't feel well, you aren't in a position to do your best work. Even if you do a stellar job anyway, those around you will believe you could have done even better if you hadn't been sick. So, no matter how great a job you do, it won't really get its due.

Wellness is the linchpin of success.
Managing it is your choice.

Getting a cold or the flu or some other temporary condition, although troublesome, has its life cycle. As you manage the symptoms, you can improve your ability to function, so each day you feel a bit better, and in time you have fully recovered. That's not the case when you have chronic wellness issues to handle.

When you have a condition that is protracted, you know it isn't going away any time soon, if ever. You're stuck with it. Now you have choices. Are you going to manage it aggressively to minimize its downside? Are you going to care for it only when it sidelines you—putting you on an endless wellness roller-coaster ride? Or are you going to deny or ignore it until it incapacitates you?

Of course, not all chronic conditions are the same. It's only your willingness to do what it takes to minimize their affects on your success that matters. You can decide to overcome or reduce the limiting factors of your condition or you can succumb to it. You can build your identity around your affliction, making sure everyone knows about it and reminding them how difficult it is for you. Or you can go about your business, performing to your greatest capability, without any mention of your wellness issues. Unless there is a need to accommodate you in the workplace because you can't get around, there is little reason for anyone to know about most chronic conditions.

If you have high blood pressure, you need to manage that. If you have diabetes, arthritis, colitis, carpal tunnel, early stages of multiple sclerosis, migraine headaches, or asthma, you have a variety of options for managing these conditions so that they don't negatively affect your ability to perform well and succeed. Yes, you will have to be dedicated to taking the mitigating steps to control the effects of these conditions. But when you make this choice, you choose to build your foundation for a successful future by maximizing your ability to feel good. You take control of the health condition that threatens to limit you.

Athletes pride themselves on staying "healthy." More often than not, they use that word to mean avoiding injury. Aside from those necessarily oversized linemen, most professional athletes work hard to keep themselves lean, strong, fast, and flexible. If this weren't a priority, why would so many of them hire personal trainers? Why would they spend so much time in the workout room? Why would each team have full time trainers and team physicians? Physical fitness is the foundation for success in most professional sports, just as "staying well" is a key foundation element for the business fitness you need for a successful career. When you aren't healthy in the fullest sense, you simply can't play the game as well or for as long.

There are thousands of people who have proven that health issues can be managed so that their careers can flourish. Many people simply won't let a chronic wellness problem stop them. In my own experience, there is Ron, an insulin-using diabetic since he was seventeen, who supervises a large crew of maintenance workers around the clock, working over sixty hours a week himself. Ron cares for his diabetes meticulously and always has, so that it won't affect his level and quality of performance. He has pursued the kind of success that would create a great life for himself and his family. Diabetes wasn't going to interfere with that.

Margaret had debilitating migraines, the kind that brought on waves of nausea at work and, at times, were so bad that she literally couldn't get out of bed. She never uttered a word of complaint about how bad she felt but simply did her job. Margaret's aggressive pursuit of treatments to minimize the negative episodes was ongoing. Her commitment to producing high quality work was never compromised. She was always regarded in the workplace for her impeccable work products rather than for the physical condition that she kept in the background. Margaret chose to manage her condition rather than being controlled by it.

How to Stay Well

You are the only one who knows how you feel. You also know the relationship between the choices you make and the way you feel. Some people may seem to have an easier time feeling well then you do, but that has nothing to do with the choices that you should make day to day. Wellness is all about you.

**It is always better to choose a healthy path
than to invite an unhealthy one.**

Every time my Dad called me at college, his first question was, "Are you taking your vitamins?"

My answer was always the same, "No, Dad. I don't need vitamins."

Then Dad would repeat a line that he was famous for all his life. "Well, that's okay so long as you have your health."

Unfortunately, my dad didn't have his health. As a matter of fact, he had so many body malfunctions from the time he was in his twenties that, when it wasn't catastrophic, he made it a laughing matter. The "did you take your vitamins" question was one way he kidded me while trying to teach me at the same time. It wasn't really a question about vitamins; it was a question about health and wellness.

Remember, staying well is a private move. It's about what you do to preserve wellness on your own. When you take actions to stay well, you are putting positive health capital into your own private account. The challenge of staying well is different for everyone and it changes as we move through time. However, there are five key factors that help you stay well:

- Get sufficient sleep regularly
- Eat a healthy diet and get some daily exercise
- Manage health conditions consistently
- Be positive about the way you think and talk to yourself
- Schedule weekly time for enjoyment

We have a tendency not to spend enough time sleeping. In recent years there has been much written about American sleep deprivation and its effects. Many of us have experienced those scary drowsiness episodes while driving—the startling head bobs while speeding down an open highway. We've struggled through those mid-afternoon business meetings where we fight to keep our eyes open during the boss's quarterly financial review. It's when these reactions are commonplace—when we experience them in some form every day—that we need to recognize that lack of sleep is hampering us.

When we aren't well rested, we aren't mentally sharp. We don't pick up on the details the way we should. We have a difficult time innovating or sustaining complex thinking. We experience a decline in energy and a loss of our vitality. When lack of sufficient sleep is protracted, we compromise our ability to resist getting sick; we become short-tempered and perhaps uncooperative; and we lose our edge. I'm not naïve. I realize that many sleep-deprived people do things to counteract their sleepiness—lots of caffeine, over-the-counter aids to stay awake, and sugar. But this approach doesn't make you business fit—it ultimately erodes your energy and your ability to build and sustain the momentum you need to reach the success you really want.

Experts talk at length about diet and exercise and their positive effects on our short and long-term wellness. There are plenty of books on how the right foods give you sustained energy and mental clarity. You need to know about that and if you don't want to read, you should talk to a physician or nutritionist. It's important to realize that everything you put in your mouth breaks down into its chemical components. Those chemicals have an effect on you, so you should understand how what you eat is affecting you chemically. Since those chemical components can trigger physical reactions, even overt behavior, you need to understand that also. So please do enough research to help you make good eating decisions for yourself.

By now you understand the importance of managing your health conditions and developing positive self-talk as you move through the challenges and experiences of each day. So the final element of staying well is one that too many people overlook. That's the importance of personal time for enjoyment. Now I'm not talking about going on vacation each year, although that's a great thing to do. I'm talking about downtime when you are not working or thinking about work. This is the time for mental rejuvenation—so it doesn't matter whether you take an hour to read a novel, play a round of golf, go antiquing, or add to your wine collection. It's time when you decouple your mind from your work.

That said, I will tell you that the value of this discipline of enjoyment is twofold. It will contribute to your overall physical and mental health because it will help you relieve stress and rekindle an awareness that you have an identity beyond your work. You will also discover that, because you are not thinking about work, your subconscious mind is. It is processing information from your enjoyment time in the context of problems or issues that you have been grappling with at work. So the next time you're in the shower or driving to the pro shop or cutting the grass, you will likely come up with a key insight for work that would not have come to you if you hadn't taken time out for yourself. My guess is that you may already have had one of these experiences even without a lot of down time. Just think of how many more of these ideas would come to you if you gave your business mind a little rest each day.

Enjoyment time has other benefits. It settles you and it connects you with family and friends in a way that deepens your connection. Even if you are simply reading a book in your easy chair, it tells them that you are a part of their world and not all about work. It is never healthy to be one-dimensional. Think of the people you have known and heard about who, upon retirement, were completely lost. They had no identity beyond their position at work, so when they retired they felt empty and meaningless. Too often we hear that these people die shortly after retirement. Making time for enjoyment and for pursuing interests that connect you with other people, reminds you that you are more than your work. That notion refreshes your thinking and enables you to look at things from a different perspective. The more perspectives that we develop and appreciate, the more likely we are to draw on them at work in ways that are unique and innovative.

The criteria for staying well are certainly not very complicated, but they do require your attention—a little each day. Here's what can happen when we let conditions at work overcome us and we fail to follow these simple wellness principles.

The Cast: Rising from the Ashes

Cliff Black's rise to district vice president seemed to be the icing on his career cake. As a successful plant manager, he took virtually no time off for sickness in almost thirty years, so he knew he had the energy and stamina for his new assignment. His career history read like a classic corporate ladder-climbing story with each promotion offering increased levels of authority and accountability.

It didn't take long before Cliff realized that a district office was a different kind of animal from a production plant. There were so many internal and external political issues swirling around him that he hardly knew where to start. As you know, the stress of these demands undid Cliff. Because Cliff was not prepared for his vice president assignment and because he didn't or couldn't manage the stress the job put on him, he crashed and burned at work. Interestingly, after Cliff was allowed to retire, he fully restored his health and continued to live a vital and happy retirement. When Cliff became free from the job he wasn't ready for, he recommitted himself to staying well and was justly rewarded for his efforts. Like Cliff, we are also in a position to turn poor health into renewed wellness. We simply need to choose feeling good first and then build from there.

In a Nutshell

Whether or not we like it, we become known for the things that we do and the things that befall us. Wellness is one of those. If we want to find success in business, we need to stay well because it's one way we will be known.

"Look at Mary," people say. "She's never missed a day of work."

"How about that Barry! He's the most dependable guy in the department—always there when we need him, always giving 110 percent. Where would we be without him?"

Being well and seeming well are two different things. It is best to be both. Staying well is the platform that you build through your choices. It gives you the legs you need to build the success you want. If you are dedicated to doing what it takes to maximize your wellness, the other steps to your business fitness will become so much easier.

YOUR PRIVATE MOVES INVENTORY: STAY WELL

The first step to getting business fit is to take stock of where you are right now. The findings in this inventory become the beginning of your *plan of action* for staying well. Once you assess your answers here, take the next step and commit yourself to doing more to stay well.

List five things you do *every day* to stay well in body and mind. Use specific action words. (Example: take a multivitamin with extra calcium, walk for 30 minutes, meditate for 20 minutes, eat one piece of fresh fruit or a salad.) List the five new things that you will do.

DO	PLAN TO DO
1.	1.
2.	2.

3.   3.

4.   4.

5.   5.

List five things you want/need to do to improve your feeling of well-being. Use specific action words. (Example: play
doubles tennis three times a week, increase weeknight
sleep by two hours, reassign certain household chores). List
the five new things that you will now do.

DO	**PLAN TO DO**
1.	1.
2.	2.
3.	3.
4.	4.
5.	5.

Chapter 5

STAY FOCUSED

You will achieve whatever you set out to achieve

Shudder. Yawn. Sputter. Gulp. These are four classic reactions to the question, "How are you doing with your goals this year?" I suspect you might be tempted to skip this chapter too because you're sick of hearing about this "goals" stuff. That would be a mistake. It's one thing to know about goal setting and quite another to understand and commit to the discipline of goal attainment. Successful people stay focused.

You may believe you're doing just fine with the business and personal goals you've set. I hope that's true. But my guess is that you set goals and then get distracted from them, both in your business and personal life. Somehow we all tend to let our attention shift away from what we've said we'd do, especially if our goals require us to do things that make us uncomfortable, unsure, or at risk. If this has happened to you, you really do need to read on. The second step to becoming business fit is a *relentless* focus on achieving your goals.

**It is counterproductive to set goals
if you're not committed to achieving them.**

You were probably told during your school days that you needed to set goals for yourself, specifically to finish high school, college, or grad school. You may have also set goals to attain a certain grade point average, induction into a club, a place on a sports team, or the attention of a cutie in your class. In a school setting, the framework for defining and achieving goals is pretty linear, and many kids who came before you succeeded by doing the same things you planned to do. Guidance counselors and teachers have a stake in your progress, so they direct, prod, or scare you into achievement. The behavior and support of your fellow students who also want to achieve their goals help to keep you on point. So by following the academic success model, you become well positioned to control the outcome.

Here's the cycle: Goals met. New goals set.

The goal setting process in business is driven by marketplace requirements for profitability. When goals are achieved the business grows, and when they aren't the business stalls or declines. Smart business leaders set the goals needed to ensure financial, operational, stakeholder, and employee outcomes essential for success. Then managers, supervisors, and individual workers set goals that deliver the results needed to achieve business goals. This too is a linear process, even though achieving goals in one part of the business may depend on the goal performance of another.

**You don't know the final score
until you've completed the game.**

Did you ever see three eight-year-olds challenge each other to a foot race? One boy says, "I can beat all of you to that old oak tree."

"Let's see," say the other two.

"On your mark. Get set. GO!" they squeal.

Half way to the tree, it's pretty clear that the challenger is way ahead of the other two. One kid keeps running anyway. The other kid quits running and yells, "Forget, it. I'm not running in your stupid race. You got a head start anyway. I saw you. This race isn't fair."

At the start the three kids shared the same goal: to see who was the fastest in this foot race. Both the winner and loser were committed to the goal, accepting either victory or defeat by completing the challenge. The third kid gave up when he believed he couldn't achieve his goal, even though a lot of things could have happened to change the outcome. The front-runner could have fallen or gotten a stomach cramp and slowed down. The boy running second might have seemed to be a contender but could have also faltered. Each kid started with a commitment to winning the race, but only two had the courage to see it through to the end. Those two learned something about themselves from the experience. The boy that stopped was willing to sign on to the goal but unwilling to see it through. As a result, he never knew whether he would have achieved it or how he stacked up to his competition. He was a double loser.

**The goals you set state what you want.
The goals you achieve show what you got.**

The only way to succeed in a big way is to stay focused on your goals. Like any private move, staying focused is something that you do each day in the quiet of your own mind. This means that you keep your goals fresh in your thinking and that you take some action every day, no matter how small, that contributes to one or more of your goals. Staying focused is a discipline—a word that most people shrink from.

Think about what professional athletes declare at the beginning of every season: "Our goal is to win the Championship." Even teams without impressive player rosters focus on this lofty goal because, if they don't, the players won't be motivated to play with passion and a commitment to continuous improvement. As the season progresses and teams fall out of Championship contention, they play on in preparation for next year's goal—to win the championship! Just because the ultimate goal isn't reached in one cycle doesn't mean that it is a goal abandoned. Athletes stay focused, year in

and year out, changing teams, improving their conditioning and capabilities, always with that championship
goal as their target. These athletes have the discipline
to stay focused and a plan to propel them.

**Goals test our capabilities and our commitments.
Achieving them is one way we define ourselves.**

To stay focused you need a plan with timetables.
Simply put, you will be more likely to stick to goals that
declare you will complete something specific. In order
to complete the goals that you have declared, you need
a plan. A plan describes the actions you intend to complete by a specific date. Actions create momentum.
Momentum builds on itself and propels you to take
more actions. The more actions, the more progress on
your plan and, *voila,* you complete your goals. Those
completed goals motivate you to set the next genera-
tion of goals and move you closer to the success you
want. The process isn't hard but the discipline to stay
focused can be.

Goals are part of your preparation. The successes you have in attaining your goals build your
energy, motivation, and commitment, adding to your
readiness to take on more challenges. The discipline of
staying focused is affected by the way you state your
goals and the way you build your plan.

**If you don't write your goals down,
they don't really exist.**

You can argue all you want about why the goals
you have in your head are just as good as if you'd

written them down. And I'll tell you that the goals you have in your head get modified each time you think about them—assuming that you do—without your ever knowing it. If you don't write down your goals, you're just plain chicken. Unwritten goals are nothing more than empty promises to yourself and to people who have a stake in you. Unwritten goals mean you are unwilling to stand up and be counted, are afraid to be accountable, and are vague and ambiguous about what you want. That may sound harsh, but it's important that you understand the importance of discipline and focus. It is your most powerful tool for making the right things happen for you.

If you want to succeed, you have to commit to measures of success. If you want to own a successful business, be promoted to vice president, earn $100,000 a year, become the go-to person on technology decisions, or retire by age forty, you need to have very specific goals, a workable plan, and a commitment to stay focused. It takes a certain amount of courage to write down your goals because they make you confront your strengths and shortcomings. When you succeed you feel good and when you don't you may feel embarrassed, discouraged, and deflated.

There is no downside of failing to achieve a goal if you take the time to understand why. More often than not, the reason you fell short is that you didn't stay focused on it. You may have written a goal that wasn't specific enough, too lofty for the time available to achieve it, or beyond your capabilities. When that's the case, consciously or unconsciously, you tend to avoid that goal because, deep down, you have a sense that it is unachievable. So the key is to start by writing effective goal statements that are challenging but achievable so you can stay focused on them.

Goals target results, not effort.

No one will argue that you have to exert effort to achieve your goals, but sometimes good fortune clears the way and your goals are met with minimal effort. The power of focus has a way of putting you in the right place at the right time in those instances. Other times life isn't quite so kind and you have to sweat every step of the way, burdening yourself with doubts about your likelihood of success.

The cold hard truth is that you earn no points for effort—admiration maybe, but no points. If a basketball player blocks five shots, makes twenty points, and grabs eight rebounds, but his team is outscored by the opposing team, his goal was not met although his effort was outstanding. When a quarterback in a tied game throws a last second, Hail-Mary pass into the end zone and his guy catches it, his goal is met even though his effort may be as much about luck as talent. The bottom line in both scenarios is that at the end of the season, the front office and the news reporters will report on outcomes, results, and achievements—with only a nod to effort.

Too often in business, people write performance goals that focus on intent not results. Don't let that happen to you. You don't build and sustain momentum through intent. Momentum comes from results—getting things done—making things happen—turning an idea into reality. A focus on goals is a focus on measurable and observable outcomes.

Think about the goals that you have in your mind right now—goals that you know can lead you to the kind of success you want. Now test them to see if they are about results more than effort:

> Are they specific?
> Are they measurable or observable?
> Have you set a date for completion?

Let's say you have a business goal that says: "Maintain control over budgeted expenses." You feel pretty good about this goal because you know that the company is in cost-control mode and that your manager is under a lot of pressure to reduce costs. But what does that goal really say? What does it mean to "maintain control"? Does it mean you intend to do what you did last year in terms of budget management even though there are new challenges to reduce costs? Does it mean that you will read the monthly budget reports more carefully, and if so, to what end?

The point here is that goals need to be specific. That's how you stay focused on results and determine the effort you need to exert to get those results. Let's say we rewrite that business goal like this: "Increase quarterly production output by 5 percent while operating at a minimum of 10 percent under budget." Now you've got something to get your blood pumping. You're committed to several measurable factors here: 5 percent increased production achieved at 10 percent below budget each quarter. Your focus now is on output, cost, and time: You set yourself up to be clearly accountable for results. You've put yourself in position to keep score and manage effort to achieve that score.

Now let's try a softer goal—one that focuses on professional development. Every business worth its salt needs employees willing to build their knowledge and skills, and all employees need to commit to their professional growth to optimize their success options. As a result, many companies ask employees to write a professional or personal improvement goal each year. Here's a development goal typical of what employees write: "Attend a workshop to improve public speaking skills." As written, this is another goal about effort, not results. The effort is "attend"—which generally means go, sit, and participate in an instructor-led training session. There is no commitment in this goal to any initiative or result after attending the training.

Here's what an outcomes-focused goal would look like: "Develop and showcase improved public speaking skills by attending a one-day, interactive training workshop and delivering a formal presentation to department leadership within three months of the training." This goal makes a commitment to skills transfer within a specific time frame. The training result will be seen in the presentation, and the employee's boss will be in a position to give specific feedback on whether or not skills have been improved.

Whether you are looking for a new job, starting your own business, building your business, seeking additional educational credentials, or exploring new career options, you need to write specific, doable, and measurable or observable goals that keep you focused on results.

GOAL STATEMENTS

Situation	Goal Statement
New Job Search	Develop a quality résumé by (date) and respond to 2 internal job postings in the next 2 months.
Starting Your Own Business	Complete a draft business plan by (date) and meet with the Small Business Administration for input in (month).
Building Your Business	Increase gross revenue from Products A and B by 10% during the June-August period through special promotions that increase customer traffic.
Expand Educational Credentials	Enroll in an on-line degree program in (course of study) and complete 6 credits with a grade of B or better by year end.
Pursuing a New Career	In the next 60 days, meet with a minimum of 9 people in careers that interest me and develop a next-steps plan.

Effectively run organizations focus relentlessly on goals that are set from the top down at the beginning of the fiscal year. Success is a function of getting everyone in the organization focused on the priority outcomes that will serve the needs of the business. When you and I, as employees, have a solid set of specific goals to achieve each year, we increase our control (our choices) over how we direct our efforts. We know that if we deliver the outcomes promised in our goals, we feel personally successful and position ourselves to be rewarded monetarily, by promotion, or by regard.

Well-crafted goals can do a lot of good. They can:

- Reduce stress because now we know what is expected of us
- Position leaders to inspire and motivate based on achievement
- Create momentum and a platform for creativity
- Build confidence and focus
- Develop a tolerance for change since new goals continue to stretch us
- Clarify accountabilities

Goals are a leader's most powerful tool for success.

When it comes to *your* success in business or in life, you are the leader. You are the one who defines the reality of your life just as business leaders define reality for their companies. You are the one who sets the direction of your choices every day. So your goals are *your* most powerful tool for achieving the success you want.

Goals for business generally fall into four categories. The following chart illustrates them and the sample performance priorities that would fall under them:

Financial	Operations
Budget management	Product production
Profitability	Service delivery
Shareowner value	Quality
Cost management	Process designs
Pricing	Competitiveness

Stakeholders	Employees
Customer acquisition	Selection and Retention
Customer retention	Satisfaction
Stakeholder satisfaction	Development
Relationship building	Compensation and Benefits

You've heard the expression: "Keep your eye on the ball." If you don't watch the ball in golf, you either end up swinging and missing or dangling a mangled wad of dirt and grass from the end of your club. If you don't keep your eye on the ball in basketball, you'll miss a pass under the basket and the chance for an easy layup. If you don't in football, you'll miss the chance to jump on a loose ball fumbled by the quarterback. Sure, sometimes we get away with not watching the ball. If the ball doesn't come our way, then it doesn't matter. But when it does and we're not tuned in, we feel the sting of a lost opportunity for a long time.

Our goals are that ball. If they are written vaguely, we can't see them, so we'll always miss opportunities. If they are written clearly, they will be more likely to keep our attention. When we don't have our goals in our line of sight, we'll miss opportunities to make progress—opportunities that may make the road easier and shorter. The truth is that goals matter. If you want to be successful, you need them. If you want to be successful in this lifetime, you must stay focused on them.

The Cast: Those Cooks That Watched the Pot

Remember the Cooks—those two school teachers that started a restaurant? These two people started with crystal clear goals that they followed with a specific plan that allowed for a healthy measure of improvisation (that's code for surprises).

Their goal was to open a gourmet restaurant with limited seatings (two rounds per evening) and limited hours four days a week. They intended to serve a professional crowd interested in creative culinary experiences with a theatrical flair in a relaxed country inn atmosphere. They fully intended to be profitable and set their prices accordingly.

The Cooks stuck to their vision but were wise enough to spot other related opportunities, like catering private parties on-site when they were closed to the public, conducting specialty nights during selected holidays, participating in high visibility community events where they could showcase some of their food specialties.

As a result, the Cooks built a business that fit them and excited their customers. They did not change their goals during those times when they were struggling to get started or when the economy took a downturn. They were committed to the vision that their goals defined. Sure they made adjustments when they had to but without abandoning their plan. They set themselves up for success by building strong goals and staying focused on them.

Be Thou a Master of Your Own Destiny

Julia Masters was on a fast track to nowhere in a steno pool right out of high school. No plan, no direction, and no dreams generally result in abject disappointment about our lives as the years go by. It's frightfully difficult to build momentum without a sense of direction. And direction comes from focus. Once Julia uttered the magic words to her boss, "I'm interested in accounting," she had found the germ of her focus. All you need is a sense of direction to get started, not the entire atlas. From Julia's insight into her own interests, she was able to develop a plan to pursue it— achievement of a college degree.

The beauty of focus on concrete goals is that it builds on itself. For Julia that undergraduate degree led to an M.B.A. and then a C.P.A.. Aligned career opportunities were uniquely tied to that learning. Knowledge and skills were the launching pad for Julia's career and she was the rocket.

There's a Pony In Here Somewhere

The eerie thing about goals is that sometimes they start out as dreams. Then they turn into options before presenting themselves as outcomes that we can achieve. When I was eight years old, I found a saddle that my mother had kept in the attic—a relic of a time when her father had kept a couple of horses. I loaded that saddle into my wagon, and with my friend, Kathy, we went around our small town saddling up more low-hanging tree limbs than you could count. All I could do was dream about horses, watch horses in cowboy movies, and gaze longingly at horses grazing whenever the family went for a country drive. That said, my parents made it clear: There would be no real horses for me in my girlhood world. That was that.

Life goes on. When I taught school, I had the summers off, so I decided to take horseback riding lessons at a stable nearby. I was in my glory. Before too long, I was riding horses for boarders when they went on vacation, and the horse bug got deeper under my skin.

When I left teaching to enter the corporate world, my horse ownership dreams turned into horse ownership goals. In time I bought my first horse and boarded it. The more I learned about horsemanship and horse sports, the more inspired I was to do more.

So I set a goal to purchase a farm where I could start a small breeding operation. (Yes, I wrote it down and revised it a few times until what I really wanted became clear.) Three years later, I found the right place and for the next seventeen years, I bred, raised, and sold thoroughbred horses commercially for the racetrack and the showring.

I share this story with you for two reasons: first, to encourage you to set goals that turn your deepest desires into reality and to stay focused on them. The second reason is to debunk the myth that you need to know everything there is to know about something before you do it. When I started in the horse business, I knew nothing about handling or foaling horses, nothing about running a farm, and nothing about the economics of breeding. Goals for learning are as important as goals for doing.

Making big things happen takes time. Sometimes making little things happen takes time. Patience and perseverance are a powerful pair, made more powerful by specific, measurable goals designed to drive results.

In a Nutshell

Your goals set the foundation for your business fitness. Everything you do is impacted by the goals that you have set for yourself and the goals that you are expected to achieve for the organization you are in. If you are reading this and saying to yourself, "I don't have any real goals for my work life (or my personal life for that matter) and I have no idea what results my boss is looking for from me," then you need to get started.

Keep in mind that your job description (if you have one) does not tell you the results you are expected to achieve this year or any other year. It will summarize duties (effort) not outcomes. If your management hasn't given you any direction on the results they expect of you this year, write your own and make them mean something. Then have a meeting with your boss and ask for input and ultimately approval. Now you will have something clear to focus on, may very likely be recognized for your initiative, and might even spark a goals focus in your boss.

Now do the same thing for yourself, setting some knowledge/skill development goals for yourself, perhaps a career goal, and some personal lifestyle goals. Write your goals down and post them somewhere at your desk or at home where you see them every day or week. Write an action plan for each goal (see Appendix B), so that you do something, no matter how minor, every day.

Then watch your momentum and your progress. One day you'll wake up and be exactly where you dreamed you would be and successful to boot!

PRIVATE MOVES INVENTORY: STAY FOCUSED

The second step to getting business fit is to focus on your specific business goals. Before you can write goals, you need to understand what you want and where you are in your business life. Use your answers to these questions to clarify your direction. Then begin to write goals that will help you to move forward.

1. In one sentence answer, "What business/role am I in (or want to be in)?" or "What do I contribute to the business that I work for?"

2. Write one sentence stating what you personally want from your business life.

3. Describe how you know when you are successful in your business life.

4. State how close you are (in months/years) to achieving what you want.

5. Describe the most significant obstacle(s) you face.

6. Write three to five specific, measurable/observable goals, including the time frame, that will move you closer to the success that you seek.

Chapter 6

STAY CURRENT

Knowledge and skills position you for success

Hopefully, this doesn't describe you: A promotional opportunity arises; you apply and don't get the job. You ask the hiring manager, "Why?" He or she says, "The successful candidate had more knowledge and experience than you did."

You say, "What do you suggest I do, Mr./Ms. Hiring Manager, to better position myself for this kind of promotion in the future." The answer, "Get an M.B.A."

I spent a decade as a senior manager in a human resources department working with managers at every level on candidate selection. After that, as a senior operating manager, I hired or participated in the hiring of dozens of management level employees. So here's the truth: Hiring decisions are likely to be influenced by your formal education; promotions are not. Unless the business you work for has a fraternity mentality, where certain credentials like an M.B.A. or degrees in specific technical disciplines are a right of passage, there is no need for you to collect academic or technical credentials to position yourself for promotion. What you need to do is know your business inside and out, acquire specific knowledge and skills needed for the jobs you want, and accumulate frontline experience—the kind that puts your knowledge and skills to the test.

Clearly there are jobs that require certifications that allow you to "practice" your trade, like being a C.P.A. (certified public accountant) or P.E. (professional engineer). These certifications give you license to approve documents and plans that must pass the scrutiny of regulators or outside agencies. I'm not talking about these credentials. What I am debunking is the notion that all the knowledge and skills you need to be successful in your career are somehow nestled in thirty hours of advanced academic degree work.

I worked for ten years in public education and have a master's degree. I am a huge supporter of the disciplines, rigor, and value of formal education. I don't have to tell you that education is the foundation of all that you do and much of what you have already become in your life. For both of us, our education started from our earliest cognition and has grown in its own fashion from the people who have made up our life communities: parents, relatives, neighbors, friends, enemies, teachers, advisors, church, employers, co-workers, and customers. Our learning has come from literally everywhere, both consciously and unconsciously. Hopefully, we also spend some time teaching ourselves by thinking about the meaning of our experiences.

Success in business is only partially rooted in our formal educational training. Success is as much about how we've applied our education, our nature, and our values to our jobs as it is about what textbooks, the internet, and teachers have put before us. Formal education and skills training is, at best, a jump start for what we will come to know and what we will do with that knowledge. The reality is that a jump-start doesn't take us anywhere unless we put ourselves in gear, set a course of direction, press the accelerator, and drive.

The key to work-life and business independence is elasticity—the more you can do or offer, the more options you have.

Knowledge and skills are the currency you use to achieve the success that you want. First, you need to figure out the knowledge and skills that have the greatest value where you work or want to work. Then you assess what you have versus what you need to build the capabilities that are valued. Remember, you want to make moves that will bring you the kind of success that you want—success that will make you happy and fulfilled. Once you understand specifically what the gaps are between what you need and what you have, then you start the process of building your capabilities.

Staying current helps you accumulate and apply information that is based on contemporary thinking and/or technical advances. It sets you apart. Sure, you may need to understand the basic principles of things like effective supervision and management, statistical methods, market analysis, and financial accounting. But, to become business fit, you need to stand out as someone who is "on top of things"—someone who can articulate emerging ideas, contemporary trends, cutting edge breakthroughs, and best practices.

Clearly, it's not enough just to know these "new and funky" things. You have to put your knowledge and skills to work—you need to incorporate your insights into the work you perform or into the information stream that is at work in your business. That may be easier said than done.

Right now, you may be reading this and saying to yourself, "Well, this all sounds good, but there's no one in my organization who is going to listen to my ideas. My boss thinks he knows it all. I don't have any idea what to do with the knowledge I'm accumulating. My job (or my constituency) is so narrow that there's no avenue to influence new ways of doing things. And I'm sure I'd be laughed at if I expressed new thinking." Did I get all of the obstacles? If not, just add them in the margin!

You're right. Regardless of size, many organizations aren't particularly conducive to encouraging idea sharing, even though, as employees, we are frequently valued or devalued based on how current (and creative) we are perceived to be. Frankly, you are probably the only one who really knows what the essential capabilities are for success in your job—both the level of knowledge and skills required. As a result, you are in the best position to add value to yourself and your work by increasing your knowledge and skills through your own efforts.

Now let's look at the value of staying current in applied terms.

Value Tactic #1:
Understand and address the business impacts
and implications of your work.

Let's say that you are a staff professional in a medium-sized company where you analyze financial data and prepare reports reviewed by a senior manager. You've been doing this work for two years and have learned that there are weaknesses in the system that captures the data that you analyze. Sometimes the data isn't timely; the process used for supplying it is inconsistent; you question the data's credibility; and the software has become dated.

Your ability to see these weaknesses has come from your efforts to stay current on a number of levels. This is what you've done:

- You've kept an eye on the timeliness issue and developed a trend graph.
- You've identified and mapped the process of data flow and identified where data gets "stuck" and/or "contaminated."

- You've assessed the weaknesses in the current software and researched upgraded versions, building a business case that demonstrates the cost benefit of investing in the new version.

This is great work. Now where do you go with it? You start by understanding what the priorities are of your boss, specifically the issues that are most troubling for him or her at the moment. (You make the most progress when you isolate a problem and present a solution that is a hot button.) You have three avenues here to assess:

- What are the business consequences of data that is not timely?
- What are the impacts and implications of ignoring the problems in the data flow process?
- What is the economic value of upgrading the software?

Right now, you are the only one in your organization who has a finger on the pulse of these problems. You have identified them, assessed them, and then applied your knowledge and skills to developing solutions to them. Now you wait for the right moment to articulate the problem and the solution.

The mistake that many of us make is jumping the gun. We see the problem and feel compelled to rush to resolution, failing to see that problem against the backdrop of hundreds of other problems in the company. Part of staying current is keeping track of the major challenges facing the business at the moment and the priority issues facing our boss on any given day. It's important to remember that business fitness requires us to see not just ourselves as players in the business game but also the nuances and requirements of the "game" itself. Just as an athlete waits to make his move, we must wait also. Success depends on good timing.

Value Tactic #2:
Keep in tune with what's going on
in your industry and the world.

Here's a statement that captures one of the biggest complaints that business leaders have about their employees: "They lack an understanding of the 'big picture.' I can see it in the decisions they make about the way they approach their work." Business leaders need us to be aware of and ready to respond positively to new marketplace demands that are always lurking. If you are perceived as a big picture thinker, you will increase your value and likelihood for success.

It doesn't matter what kind of work you do—technical, strategic, or relational—if you know what the best practices are, how the market is trending, where the latest technologies can be found, or what customers want—you will be recognized as someone in the know, and that has real value to you and the business.

Here are some things you can do to keep yourself current on what's going on "out there."

YOUR "TO DO" LIST FOR STAYING CURRENT

Things to Do	Things to Notice
Read	
Books:	Trends
Business	
Biographies	Innovations
Nonfiction	
Fiction (You'll learn a lot	Breakthroughs
about human behavior.)	
	Popular opinion
Periodicals (Magazines	
and Newspapers):	Controversial opinion
Current events	
Business	Influential people
Trade	
Travel	Consumer behavior/preferences
Consumer	
Arts	Fads
	Change/debunked information
	Misdeeds
Listen and Observe	
Media Figures:	Points of view
Commentators	
Spokespeople	Constituencies
"Experts"	
Panels	Insights
Eye-witnesses	
	Scope and depth of
Public Figures (local, state,	perceptions
national, international):	
Politicians	Emotionality/rationality
Community leaders	
Business leaders	Crossover thinking
Educators	
Celebrities	Trends
Athletes	
	Fresh ideas
Your Personal Circle	
Friends	Contradictions
Family	
Neighbors	Alliances

Colleagues and associates
Church members   Undercurrent
Clubs members

Research

Interviewing (Talking to   Facts
People in the Know)
Industry experts (within or   Trends
   outside your organization)
Business leaders   Charts and graphs
Educators
Customers   Opinions
Suppliers
Vendors   Attitudes
Marketers
Colleagues   Issues and priorities
Government officials
                                        Concerns
Internet Sites
Technical   Suggestions for improvement
Business
Government   Processes
Management and leadership
Product   Best practices

Libraries/Archives   Historic practices
Trade associations
GSO Libraries (The U.S.   Opportunities for change
   Government Service
   Organization houses government Potential pitfalls
   published documents there.)
Your business's archives   Perceived players
   (hard copy or electronic)

Formal Learning

Academic Classes   New or expanded knowledge
(Live or Electronic)
College or trade school for credit   Technical skills
On-line
Adult education (noncredit)   Soft skills
Auditing (noncredit)
                                        Applied skills
Skills Training
Employer-offered on-site   Process models
Self-funded outside of work
Computer-aided instruction   Work improvement methods

Now, you may be looking at this list and thinking, "This isn't what I expected." It is not a list of the "right" books and magazines to read or the specific trends that all "good business people" follow. That's because this is about staying current in your field—any field—every field.

The mistake that we often make is to become so specialized in the details and strategies of the business we are currently working for that we stay current but in a narrow way. If you want to be business fit, maximizing your value and ensuring your own career flexibility, you need to develop a sense of your work, including where and how it fits into the world of business, which, these days, is becoming "the world." When you only know about the business you work for and forget the larger context of that business, which is the universe of business and society, you reduce the range of your creative thinking. We'll talk more about the importance of this in Chapter 10.

As amorphous as it may sound, staying current means staying on top of hard facts and concepts while feeding the intuitive side of your brain—a side that unconsciously absorbs impressions and perceptions and synthesizes them into new ideas when the time is right. When you go back over the "to do" list for staying current, you'll see that the "things to notice" are a combination of concrete information and abstract insights. Remember: staying current in business means knowing your product and service and understanding the needs of your customers. It means understanding the performance expectations of your boss and the culture of the workplace. It means following the chain of command and understanding the subtleties of work-place politics. To stay current on the job, you need to keep learning while holding your ear to the ground.

**Learn something new everyday;
try something new every week.**

Staying current is about knowledge (learning) and skills (doing). It's about activity done in a way that builds your capabilities—a private move. Committing to learning something new every day can be as little as scanning a periodical like the *Wall Street Journal*, watching CNBC for fifteen minutes, or listening to National Public Radio. You're just looking for one new insight every day—that's 365 insights each year. The more ideas that pass through your consciousness, the more you will assimilate those ideas until they become concepts that you can apply to your work. It really doesn't take that much time or effort—just your attention. You'll build momentum around this accumulation of ideas and that leads to action.

You build your skills in much the same way. There are tasks that you do every day at work—they can be physical or mental, technical or soft. There is always a better or more effective way to do these tasks, something we often figure out by trial and error. So take a chance. Break your patterns. See if there is a better work process that can get things done more efficiently. Try to break down a barrier with someone at work by engaging them in conversation. Build a better relationship with someone by asking them to join you for lunch. When you attend a training class, make a firm commitment to transfer at least three of the skills learned to your job by applying them rigorously at every opportunity until they are automatic, the equivalent of an athlete's muscle memory. When you apply new skills in ways that add value, you set an example of professional growth—one by-product of staying current.

This is my way of saying that you need to take charge of your capability currency by making a steady and concerted effort to build your knowledge and skills by staying current, using the same disciplined approaches you've used to stay well and focused. I'm also saying that you need to do this on your own— remember, staying current is a private move.

When you have know-how, you have leverage.

Leverage increases your ability to influence— something that is essential to your ability to find success through your public moves. (See Chapters 8 and 9.) Staying current helps you know what to do in a given situation and how to do it. When you can both "know" and "do," you have doubled your value.

The power of leverage that comes from knowledge and skills is palpable. Take for instance the human resource manager who is also the chief labor negotiator for a large company. The relationship between union and management officials, particularly during contract negotiations, is often less than pleasant. The company's concerns focus on how the union's demands will impact on the company's profitability and flexibility. The chief negotiator is accountable for delivering an affordable contract. He is the only executive who understands firsthand the union's demands and the culture of their negotiating team. He is the one who knows what will drive them to strike or get them to settle. The chief negotiator has specialized knowledge of the entire labor environment and the specialized skills for high stress, high stakes negotiating. This combination of current knowledge, skills, and insights, all of which have been tested under fire, gives the chief negotiator maximum leverage to influence the highest levels of decision making in the company. It has made him an invaluable asset, positioning him for unique opportunities and rewards.

Employees with a frontline connection with customers have a similar opportunity to increase their leverage by staying current. Companies live and die by their ability to meet the needs of their customers through both their products and services. If you are a first-line supervisor at a customer call center, you listen to customer complaints every day. You see the degree of effectiveness of your employees, the computer software they use, the reliability of the telephone system, the effectiveness of the fulfillment process, and the accuracy of the billing system. As you solve problems for customers, read about best practices at other companies, and investigate internal processes, you can develop solution options for operational problems.

Your ability to articulate the value of those solutions in terms of feedback that you receive firsthand from customers increases the likelihood that management will listen to your solutions. Even if you don't get management action the first time, your repeated scenarios, tracking and trending documentation, and case studies will establish your unique knowledge of customer needs. By demonstrating your front-line connections and understanding of the customer, you establish your ongoing value which positions you for continued success.

The driving point here is this: When you climb into trenches that others avoid and uncover truths or develop capabilities that others lack, you have increased your value. Those trenches can be intellectual, technical, and/or relational. When you know something firsthand and can speak confidently about it because you have "been there," you have developed a capability currency that has great value.

The Cast: It All Starts with Knowing

Julia Masters is all about the strength of knowledge. Just from a success perspective alone, she shows us the importance of having knowledge platforms from which to launch our work lives. For Julia getting a degree in accounting became the foundation for a career she continues to build. That knowledge base opened her mind, increased her options, positioned her for jobs and career moves that didn't stop.

Julia built knowledge momentum by taking what she learned, applying it to her work, increasing her level of knowledge (getting an M.B.A. and then a C.P.A.) and transferring it to higher level activities. She understood the building blocks of knowledge in the context of the corporation's needs. Each time she specialized in her field, she knew where that capability was needed and how she could combine it with her skills and interests.

The multiplier effect of knowledge, especially applied knowledge, enables you to maximize your value to your organization over time with decreasing effort. How nice is that!

Knowledge and Skill Is the Heart of the Matter

As you may recall, Doug Hart was a college grad with a degree in business administration who got a job in a hospital. Doug had an inquiring mind and set about to meet and talk to cardiologists about their work, particularly the new technologies and operating room procedures. The more he read and studied on his own, the more people he talked to, the more cases he followed, the more articulate and knowledgeable he became on cardiac-catheter procedures. His knowledge became so impressive that one day, a heart surgeon with whom Doug had developed a relationship, invited him to scrub in and observe a catheterization for one of his patients. That was the breakthrough for Doug.

He built on that experience and took the steps needed to become a highly regarded technician, assisting many different surgeons and developing a reputation for knowledge and skill.

It was that reputation and his frontline (operating room) experiences, both with the technology and the doctors, which led him to a successful and lucrative career years later as a sales executive for the companies that sold heart catheters to surgeons. For Doug, staying current paid off in a big way.

Many Times It Is What You Know!

As I have said, the first ten years of my professional career were spent teaching high school students.

I'd worked in two different school districts and understood the educational system, educator standards, and curriculum development.

My first corporate position was coordinator of consumer education programs for an energy company. My goal was to help teachers and students increase their energy knowledge and related consumer issues in an unbiased way.

With the support of my boss, I started to learn what the industry's public issues were on energy and what the "big picture" implications would be over successive generations of customers. With that knowledge as a base, I developed a plan that involved a broad cross section of teachers and school administrators who also saw the need for better environmental and consumer education on energy. All of this came together in a program proposal to executive leadership.

Needless to say, there were many barriers to overcome before the executive council would approve my request for funding. But there were two main factors that contributed to success: knowledge of the current issues facing the company with its publics and the leverage of my ten years of frontline experiences in education. Sure, a lot depended on communication skills, both writing and speaking, as well as the myriad of relationships and lower level support that were needed to support its implementation. But if I hadn't been able to stand before the leadership and declare that, because of my knowledge and experience, I knew how to make this program work, this project would not have gone forward.

In a Nutshell

Staying current pays off and it doesn't take much. Do a little something every day to add to your knowledge about the business of which you're a part, the business world, and the global society in which we all live. Build your skills by attending training, apprenticing, or observing others, and apply them repeatedly until they feel automatic.

Increasing your leverage will build confidence and influence. See where you can develop know-how and insights that are uniquely valuable and that place you in a position to have your finger on the pulse of your business constituencies.

Staying current is as much about staying alert, tuned in, and aware as it is about formally gathering information. The two actually work well together. The trick is to broaden your picture of the working world continuously and avoid the tendency to get mired in day-to-day tasks. Your career and your success are about growth. Staying current is valuable food for that growth—so keep eating.

PRIVATE MOVES INVENTORY: STAY CURRENT

The third step to getting business fit is to stay current—building the knowledge and skills that keep you on top of the action in the marketplace, increase your leverage, and add to your value. Use your answers to develop a daily action plan that will build insights and capabilities that you need to stay on the cutting edge of opportunity.

In each of the following categories, list one thing about your organization that you need to know more about?

- The Competition
- Customer Requirements
- Product or Service Strengths or Weaknesses
- Financial Performance
- The Strength of Your Industry
- The Culture of Your Organization
- Other

List three things you will do daily or weekly to keep informed about the local, national, and/or global marketplace:

1.

2.

3.

List three things you will do in the next twelve months to increase/improve your skills:

Skill	Action to Improve
1.	
2.	
3.	

Chapter 7

STAY CONNECTED

Develop relationships that help you navigate conditions

When I first started my consulting practice, I hired an advisor who told me that if I was going to be successful, I needed to network like there was no tomorrow. I was advised to read books on networking, which I did. I was encouraged to attend local business mixers and use the networking techniques that I'd read about. I was pressed to join any number of organizations so that I could meet lots of people who would ultimately become or lead me to clients.

So I followed that advice. I went to the mixers and walked up to people who I thought were also there to network. I followed all the techniques for introducing myself, engaging in conversation (not too long, you know, because you have to move on and meet others), and made that all-important move to exchange business cards. I followed up with people too, just like the books said. The result I got for this effort was nothing more than a lot of names stored in my address book.

I must say that I know a good number of people who believe they have been very successful because of their networking. They network because they are comfortable playing the numbers. If you meet a lot of people, ultimately the law of averages will deliver a positive business hit. And that does happen. But that kind of networking didn't work for me. The process felt artificial, and it did not provide a platform for developing relationships—something that is important to me.

People in positions of power and influence in big business generally credit their success to the relationships they have developed with employees, peers, and leaders within their organizations. That certainly had been true for me. They do the same with industry peers, community leaders, and government officials. Sure, we meet lots of people at first in group settings, but we develop relationships by working together to achieve something we believe has value.

There is a difference between the act of networking and your network. Some would say that you can't have one without the other; that may be true at some level. But networking, the act of finding and meeting people in the marketplace or within your company, does not necessarily create your network. Staying connected with people who have the knowledge, skills, and insights that you need to succeed builds a network.

> **The value of your network grows
> from the connections within it.**

Building a network is a discipline. It's a business strategy—a private move that is essential to your business fitness. Your network is the foundation upon which you build your career and your ability to produce meaningful results. It is not something that comes from making idle contacts and superficial acquaintances. It results from good choices, partnered efforts, proper information sharing, and mutual support around common objectives.

This means that you need to be selective about those you affiliate with in business and those you invite to affiliate with you. The business value of staying connected is similar to the value of relationships in sports. If you are a quarterback in football, you need to connect with your offensive linemen since they're the guys protecting you from getting sacked. If you play professional sports, you need to develop cordial relationships with the media that can help you build a positive image or cut you some slack if you don't play well. If you want to become business fit, you need to stay connected to those people who can help you achieve the kind of success that benefits you and your organization.

> **You are known by what you do,
> how you do it, and who your connections are.**

I'm sure you've heard the expression: "It's not what you know; it's who you know." Lots of people believe that "getting ahead" is simply about having a connection to people in key positions. If you know those people, you're "in" and if not, you're "out." So if you believe that to be true and you're not getting ahead, then it is pretty easy to blame your lack of success on someone else, not yourself. To become business fit, simply knowing people is not enough.

Yes, we both know or have heard of people who have gotten a leg up in business because they knew someone. Let's say you studied botany in school and know that your Uncle Rudy owns a successful landscaping company. You (or someone in your family) tell him that you'd like to work for him, and, *voila,* you have a job. At first you're just digging holes and planting shrubs, but eventually, you're running a crew, ordering inventory, and expanding the product line. Eventually, Uncle Rudy makes you a part owner and then turns the business over to you when he retires.

Chances are you've heard similar stories about how college roommates team up to start a business, get support from an alumnus, and make it big. Other times, the story is about how someone just stumbles into the path of a patron, talent scout, or hiring manager, and lands a great deal—it can be a matter of luck.

Although these circumstances could accrue to you, the odds are generally small. Banking your future on trying to figure out who you need to know and how to get to them is a low-odds strategy. With all due respect to the six degrees of separation, you can spend a lot of time trying to figure out who you need to know and discover that when you meet him or her, there is very little context from which to create a strong connection. Your business fitness is built on your ability to stay connected in a sustained and meaningful way—not by luck or happenstance, but through effort that is sincere and mutually beneficial.

I wish I had been the person who came up with this next insight, but I'm not. Because I don't know who said this, I can't even give credit to him or her. But I heard this said by a good friend of mine who is a model of staying connected:

It's not who you know: It's who knows you.

Think about it: If the people who can assist you in achieving your success goals don't know who *you* are and what you have to offer, it really doesn't matter that you know them. You may think this is just semantics and verbal sleight of hand. It's not. There's a difference between being recognized as a name or a face and being known as a doer and an ally.

Scenario #1

Imagine that you are at a chamber of commerce mixer with about three hundred business people, many of whom are company CEOs, business owners, and professionals (attorneys, C.P.A.s, bankers). As you network by "working the room," you approach half a dozen of the big players, shake hands and exchange pleasantries. The conversation lasts a few minutes until another chamber member enters the mix and you move on. In this situation, you are recognized by the people you want to know; therefore, you believe that you have taken another positive step to build your network.

Scenario #2

Now imagine yourself again at the same mixer. As you enter the room and begin to reacquaint yourself with the key players, two things happen. While you are talking with a prominent business person, he or she steers you to a more private spot so you can talk more privately about a community initiative that you are both involved in. Perhaps it's something associated with Rotary, a business-education initiative, or economic development. After you've had your private conversation and return to the larger group, another business person approaches you to talk about a chamber committee activity you are leading, an article you've written in a local publication, your score at a charity golf tournament, or your involvement on a nonprofit board. In this scenario you know people who know you because you have created and sustained a genuine connection through shared commitments, interests, and involvements. That's the kind of connection that enhances your business fitness because it has substance and showcases both your values and your capabilities.

Scenario #2 could just as easily happen at work where staying connected has more immediate and ongoing value. The next time there is a business event where executive and/or management leadership meet with employees, look around. Who are the employees that the leadership approaches? What are they talking about? What is the nature of their relationship? Where or how did it originate? You will likely find that the staff people enjoying a connection to these leaders are known for their unique contributions to the business, the quality of their performance, their willingness to share ideas, or their involvement in the community or the industry. They have, in some way, demonstrated value to these leaders and have become known for what they contribute.

In Scenario # 1 you are a face to the people you believe you need to know. In Scenario #2 you are recognized as a player, contributing value to the business initiatives supported by the people you want to know you. The best way to build and cement a business relationship within and outside your company is to showcase what you can do as a leader, manager, or technical specialist. That's how the "right people" get to know *you* and what you "bring to the party." The more ways you connect to the initiatives that drive business momentum, the more you will likely find yourself in the line of sight of the movers and shakers in your company or business community.

**The coach won't put you in the game,
if he or she doesn't know you can play.**

Every sports team has starters and bench players. Week after week the whole team practices together. The coach knows each and every player by the time the season begins. Even though you're on the team, you may sit on the bench for many of the games, but each week you continue to work out and practice with your teammates. Even though you don't get to play, you watch films, improve your conditioning, encourage your teammates, and celebrate the great play of the starters. You ask insightful questions about game strategies and seek out opportunities to do drills with teammates who are rehabilitating injuries. You stay connected with the team's goals, the coach's scheme, the needs of your teammates, as well as the boosters and the team's fans by supporting their efforts. When a starter that plays your position gets hurt or ejected from the game or when the score means the nonstarters will get to play, you have positioned yourself to be the one the coach calls for.

It's not enough just to keep up your skills—anyone can do that. You have to be recognized as someone who cares about the outcome, not for yourself alone but for all the people who will be impacted by it. Staying connected is not about simply staying in touch—it's about being engaged and personally invested in the effort. It's about contributing your support, time, effort, and personal resources in a meaningful and ethical way. Staying connected is about building and sustaining solid relationships in the workplace, industry, and community that wraps around the stakeholders (i.e., customers/clients, shareowners, allies, vendors, regulators, and contributors) who are affected by what you do.

Your connections are your power base.

Success in business is a function of the quality and depth of the relationships that you build. When you have strong, positive relationships both vertically and horizontally in your business organization, you increase your ability to influence decisions, anticipate change, detect misinformation, achieve desired results, and position yourself and others to move forward.

**Myth: Power is solely a function of
your position in the organization.
Truth: Power is an enduring by-product
of your relationships.**

Job titles come and go, but your business relationships last a long time. When two businesses merge, what tends to happen? The business that is bought out generally sees the exodus of its leadership. And why is that? Because those leaders aren't connected with the decision makers from the company buying them out. The leaders that get to stay either have unique expertise or have had a prior relationship that carried over from their industry involvements.

The power of staying connected is equally as significant on a day-to-day basis in a company that is quite stable—a company where you can grow professionally, organizationally, and financially. Too often, we are led to believe that our candidacy for promotion is a function mainly of our knowledge and skills when it is the quality of our relationships that truly positions us to move up.

**Your connections are your leverage
and your safety net.**

The misconception about staying connected is that it is about looking "up" the organization and building relationships there. That's a flawed strategy because it's lopsided. You need to build relationships with good people in every area of your organization—that means among employees in your own and other departments, with your peers across the board, and with the leadership across functions. Remember what you read about staying current in Chapter 6. The realities of business life are more than what you read in the company newsletter. The inside track on what's going on comes from the people—both frontline and management—who are in the thick of things. That knowledge only comes to you if you have stayed connected. When you are "in the know," you have the knowledge that will help you position yourself to make good choices—ones that will contribute to your success and benefit the organization.

Develop a broad base of allies: be an ally.

The best relationships are based on mutual regard, so your efforts to stay connected should be focused on relationships rooted in integrity, mutual respect, and a shared commitment to doing the right things in the right way. The alliances you build this way create a lasting bond because they are built on values that are unwavering. Each party knows they can count on the other because they share principles that are solid.

Help Comes From Unlikely Sources

Positive connections that help your career and your success can come from surprising places. If you want to build those connections, you need to see who people are rather than their place on the organization chart.

**Good connections inform you of
potential trouble in time for you to respond.**

My first corporate career change moved me from the marketing department to management training. I was relocated from the high-rise, urban headquarters to a beautiful training center located on fifty pastoral acres outside the city, a site originally established to conduct technical training for frontline personnel. Management training wasn't held in particularly high regard by the staff out there since the subject matter was "all that soft stuff." Nonetheless, everyone got along just fine.

In the course of things, the director of the facility was reassigned, and ultimately I replaced him. All of a sudden, I was a nontechnical manager, operating this technical facility, replete with welding shop, transportation garage, and practice yards for skills labs. This job also came with responsibility for the physical plant—grounds maintenance, sewage tank pumping (yes, the dreaded "honey dipper"), building security, and facility repairs.

Before I was tapped for this interesting assignment, I had developed a positive working relationship with the lead building mechanic assigned to the training center. He was an extraordinary talent, able to design and implement complex fixes that involved plumbing, electrical applications, and carpentry. There was literally no part of overseeing a facility that he couldn't handle. On top of that, he held himself to the highest standards of performance, both in quality and timeliness.

I always admired how he worked and the fine example he set for others—both the management and union employees. Whenever the opportunity presented itself, I would ask him about his trade and his attitudes about work. We became fast friends and respected colleagues, each understanding and respecting the part we played in the company, while recognizing that we both were committed to doing high quality work because it was the right thing to do.

Our connection was rooted in shared values. We understood that the way we worked could have a real benefit on the way the company performed, setting an example for others. When I was promoted to training center director, there were rumblings among some of the technical people there. They questioned my credibility to lead the organization but never to my face. My building mechanic friend heard those comments and shared them with me along with strategies to address them. He helped me establish myself in this rather foreign environment by keeping me current on morale and by voicing his personal views about my capabilities with those doubting me. We supported each other throughout our careers, even when we weren't in the same departments, contributing to the kind of success we both wanted and a lasting friendship.

Nothing Beats a Net Once You've Run Out of Rope!

The connections that you make among your colleagues throughout your organization provide you with the information needed to navigate the day-to-day demands of your work. It is true, though, that your "friends in high places" are often the only ones who can help when you have run out of options.

Senior executive connections are unique and hold high value. They tend to evolve from work that you've done and had showcased for this audience as part of the company's interest in developing future leaders. Sometimes executive connections come from community or industry involvements. Generally, they grow from exposure to the consistent, quality work that you perform and the spirit with which you perform it. Executives understand fully the strings that only they can pull to make things happen; you need to understand that too. Before you ask for help from your executive connections, however, you need to demonstrate that you have tried every possible alternative available to you.

When I was a marketing manager, I worked for a man who met most requests from his direct reports with a "no" response. In spite of the fact that I'd had a major program proposal approved by the CEO and his senior executive team, this boss wouldn't approve any of my initiatives regardless of their value. I was at my wit's end.

During my years in marketing, I had done considerable work with a vice president in another department—work that took us among employees and community groups, responding to a variety of sensitive community issues that involved the company. We had developed a mutual respect and regard. Our respective departments reported to the same executive vice president, a man who had been the vice president of the marketing department when I started there. So I had a strong connection with him too.

At the height of my anger and frustration with Mr. "No," I called my VP friend and vented with a personal fire he had never heard before. I had to do something but didn't know what. I couldn't afford to quit nor did I want to, but I thought that was my only option left. Here's how the conversation went:

"Can you give me five minutes to make an arrangement for you," he said.

"Sure. Thanks for listening to me. I'll wait for you to call me back."

Five minutes pass.

I answer the phone and hear these words from the VP, "I'm offering you an equivalent manager level job in my department fully approved and effective immediately. Now go to Mr. No's VP and tell him that you can no longer work for him. You've got nothing to lose. Good luck."

Can you imagine how that felt? To have the support and faith of two highly regarded officers, willing to confront managers who were senior to me, was mind-boggling. You can imagine how my commitment and loyalty to them increased.

Well, this is how it turned out. I went to Mr. No's boss, the department VP, and explained my frustration. I never had to mention my ace in the hole. Instead the VP told me that he understood the situation and arranged to have me report directly to him from then on. Now, it may very well have been that his connections and mine had conferred before we met.

That wouldn't have mattered to me. The point is that positive connections, based on good work, right intentions, and respect are powerful assets.

**Help from your connections is a gift—
not a transaction.**

The last thing you want to do is develop connections on a tit-for-tat basis. Staying connected is more like a savings account than a checking account. You build your relationships because they feel right and you draw on them when you need to. When you ask one of your connections for advice, information, or help, you are not obligated to "pay that person back." What you must do is acknowledge that help and continue to stay connected. When someone helps you, it's a reminder that you need to help someone when called upon—that may be the person who helped you or someone else.

The way you stay connected reflects your personal style and the style of the people with whom you have developed relationships. Some relationships require more contact than others. Circumstances, distance, organizational levels, work requirements, and time are the usual factors that affect the way we stay connected. Here are some suggestions:

WAYS TO STAY CONNECTED

Get together for lunch (You have a lunch hour; use it to maintain connections.)

Make periodic "checking in" phone calls or send e-mails

Arrange to meet at a company or community event and sit together

Follow up on announcements: promotions, awards, progress on projects, family events (weddings, births, graduations)

Share information (articles, white papers) on areas of interest, both professional and personal

Request input and/or get feedback on ideas, projects, and initiatives that align with their expertise

Invite them to serve on a project team with you, make a presentation, or provide expertise

Share perspectives on company and industry direction that you believe to be of value to them

Send notes and/or cards on holidays

Send greetings to them through mutual acquaintances

Staying connected is about staying in the loop. It is an informal process done in a conscious way. You need to spend some time each week thinking about the people that matter to you and do something for at least one of them to stay connected. Just one contact each week will touch twelve people each quarter. Generally, the more solid the relationship, the less regular contact is needed; the newer the relationship, the more you need to stay connected. Working together on a project of mutual interest is the quickest, and, in my view, the best way to build strong relationships that will have lasting benefits.

The Cast: Losers and Winners

Staying connected is the fourth of the private moves that help you build your business fitness. In your own unique and personal way, you quietly take the steps that are needed to build and maintain the relationships that enable you to move forward with your work life. When you stay well, stay focused, and stay current, you have a strong framework for your relationships. The people in your circle understand who you are, what your goals are, where your expertise lies, and where they fit in.

Remember Matt Clinger, the manager who had all those executive connections and lost them, only to end up "on ice" in a small, isolated office waiting for his early retirement package? He only built relationships "up" the organization. He demonstrated little interest in relationships with "lower level" employees. Instead of building a broad spectrum of relationships, Matt stuck with a narrow group at the top and disregarded groups at lower levels. In the end he had no one willing or able to help him.

The Cooks, on the other hand, were masters of the care and feeding (quite literally) of relationships built over decades in the classroom and in the community. The Cooks always kept in touch with former students with whom they felt a bond, so some of those ex-students spent time at the restaurant as wait staff. One from this group, after completing culinary arts school, became their chef. The Cooks maintained strong relationships with the parents of many of their students who became regular customers and brought their friends. Both of the Cooks were active in the arts community. Their network was based on long-standing, well-maintained relationships that came from their dedication to the work they did whether in the classroom or over a hot stove.

In a Nutshell

Staying connected starts with creating a relationship and then maintaining it through periodic contacts. If you like networking as a way to meet people, that's great. But, for the sake of your business fitness, take that all-important step to engage with the people you feel most aligned with by finding an activity that lets you work with them. The fastest way for people to learn about you is by working with you—and the reverse is true.

Remember, the private moves are the steps you take to position yourself for success. You want to build a network of people who share your vision, insights, and values. The right people will see where you want to go and help you get there. They may also show you that there is an even better, more rewarding path for you to follow—a path you hadn't been able to see without their help. Building positive relationships by staying connected to supportive people is a challenge. Each time you find someone who belongs in your corner, remember to keep that relationship strong by staying connected. It doesn't have to be a big move, just a meaningful one.

Now, you're ready to step out and let the business see what you can do. You're ready to develop your Public Moves—the steps that will let you showcase your capabilities. So, buckle up...you're ready to roll!

PRIVATE MOVES INVENTORY: STAY CONNECTED

The fourth step to getting business fit is to stay connected—building and maintaining positive relationships with people in business who reflect the kinds of values, integrity, work ethic, and commitment to quality performance that you do. Use your answers to identify the key people in your business life with whom you need to stay connected. Then contact those people over the next three months in a way that will enhance your relationship.

List the names and titles of your five most important business allies/relationships.

Name   **Title**

1.

2.

3.

4.

5.

List three things you can do at least quarterly to stay in contact with these people.

1.

2.

3.

List five additional business relationships you need to build that would be mutually beneficial.

Name and Title   **Organization**

1.

2.

3.

4.

5.

PART THREE

PUBLIC MOVES

Chapter 8

ATTRACT A FOLLOWING

Demonstrate your capabilities through collaboration

It's time to go public!

Once you've implemented your wellness regimen, clarified your focus, built a strong base of capabilities, and established your network, your business fitness foundation is set. All of this preparation helps to get you ready to make your public moves. You should now feel motivated, energized, and committed to go forward.

If going public makes you feed anxious, take heart. No one ever feels fully prepared or fully ready to make their public moves. Part of the excitement of a career is the adventure and the discovery. Preparation gives us the footing and readiness gives us the adrenaline to take our forward-moving steps with optimism grounded in reality. This doesn't mean that you won't be tentative about making public moves, and it doesn't mean that you won't question your preparation when things don't go as perfectly as expected. At some point, we're simply ready enough to get out there and attract attention.

Each us of gets a brand identity (or two) whether we like it or not. Successful people take steps to influence what it will be.

We're all aware of the brand identities associated with famous people like Donald Trump and Oprah Winfrey. Although each has attracted a following through different career paths, they each have a brand identity associated with their appearance, their professional achievements, and their social consciousness.

Donald Trump's brand is a composite of his notable hair style and business suit, elegant Trump buildings and recreational facilities, his "Apprentice" reality TV show, and his charitable initiatives serving the City of New York.

Oprah is famous for her on-screen style and her openness about her struggles to control her weight. The success of her television talk show and "*O*" magazine is undisputed. She has mobilized her legions of fans to join her in supporting her many charitable initiatives to create social change at home and in Africa.

Just like celebrities, we too are capable of attracting a following and may do so whether we intend to or not. The kind of success we want determines the extent and composition of the "following" that we need and want to attract. Just like celebrities, we become known and branded by how we look, the work we produce, and what we stand for on the job, in our community, and at home. How we are branded affects how we are regarded. The more engaged we are in building and managing that brand, the more we enhance our ability to achieve the success we seek. The more our brand resonates with the interests, needs, and values of others, the more likely we are to attract the kind of people who want to help us do good work.

Now it's time for a little reflection. How would you define your brand? When people hear your name, see you enter a room, or look at your work, what labels do they give to you? What has been the evolution of your brand? What have you done to manage it? Remember: you may have different brands for different "audiences" that you count among your following. So ask yourself what your brand is at home, at work, among your friends, and in the community. Then, if you feel brave, ask people who will be honest with you, how they define your brand.

At the risk of embarrassing myself, I'll give you a snapshot of the evolution of my own brand—at least as I see it— and as others have defined it for me.

The Nickname Brand

In the sixth grade, I was the tallest and, quite possibly the stoutest, kid in my classroom. In those days, when we had to go as a group to lunch or assembly, the teacher lined us up, you guessed it, by height. At the time, a cereal company was advertising its product on TV using a cartoon character called "Big Otis." Someone thought that sounded like a good "brand" nickname for me—and it stuck even after I was outgrown by the boys. Once I became less physically "big," I was still perceived as having a level of enthusiasm for things that my friends considered "big." That was a function of the big ideas and big plans I often talked about with my classmates. The point is that brands are often easier to acquire than to shed. They can arrive by default. That's why it's important to take steps to drive the brand you want instead of waiting for others to assign one to you.

The Title Brand

In college I was sorority president. A title like this is an early indication of how leadership becomes a by-product of your following. In my case this title had more to do with the needs of my "following" than it did about me.

Oddly enough, I wasn't particularly close with many of the members of my sorority. Some I barely knew. Frankly, I wasn't interested in becoming president as I saw it as a lot of administrative headache—having to organize and run meetings, oversee finances, work with alumni advisors, solve interpersonal problems with the "sisters," and handle a lot of rigmarole from National. I was elected because I had a developing brand and a following of people who considered me well-organized, principled, collaborative, fair and compassionate, while being able to make decisions that were good for the organization.

As adults we often cringe at some of the things that we did in high school and college. I certainly have. However, in my student years, there were very few extra-curricular options where young women could develop their brand in an organizational context. Fortunately, today there are many more outlets. The bottom line is that, early on, all of us need to examine and take advantage of opportunities to attract a following and then understand what the foundation of that "following" is. Ideally, your "following" will be composed of people attracted by your skills, integrity, principles, vision, and quality of work.

The Performance Brand

I contend that what you do and how you do it are the most powerful and lasting methods of attracting and maintaining your following.

As I have said, I taught high school English for ten years before I started my career in a company with an engineering focus. I often joked that when the hiring manager saw that my degrees were in "Eng.," he must have thought that meant engineering. Actually, I was hired because I was an educator and the company wanted to strengthen its relationship with the educational community. My job was to do just that, and for many years my brand there was associated with my old title—teacher.

As my career progressed and my leadership responsibilities increased, my brand started to change. Why, because I could write well—at least those engineers thought so! In fact they discovered that what I could do was to listen to a discussion of broad and complex issues (e.g., customer needs, regulatory processes, employee issues, and company strategies), find the common ground, and turn that discussion into concise written documents. That skill and my willingness to be a trusted and honest broker became an invitation to many conference tables. My brand changed too. I was never given a nickname or branded by my company titles—and I'd had many of them. I was branded by my ability to understand issues, propose initiatives and change, and then lead diverse groups to a successful outcome. When my colleagues saw me or heard my name in a business setting, these capabilities were what came to mind.

Your brand isn't something that gets stamped on your head after you finish school or get a job or buy a fancy car. For successful people it is more about who you are, and who you are is more about what you do on an ongoing basis. Going from "Big Otis" to "big company" leadership roles took me a long time, but everything builds on itself. The key is to stay focused on what kind of success you want and to stay connected with the people who will likely become your following.

Your brand is either enhanced or diminished by your following.

Remember how in "Staying Connected" (Chapter 7) the truism was "It's not who you know, it's who knows you." That's where I introduced the idea of focusing on building quality relationships. I'm sure you've heard the adage: "You are judged by the company you keep." That can be quite true. As a result, you want your following to represent connections with good people.

There is often a misconception that your following needs to be people in positions of power and influence, the business "movers and shakers," the "climbers and talkers." Remember: it's called "attracting" a following not "creating" one. You can't create a lasting and satisfying following if your relationships and collaborations don't come from a shared set of principles, intentions, and desired results.

**Attracting a following is natural and organic.
Creating a following is forced and artificial.**

Although your following will surely include people you count as your friends, it should also include relationships of diverse types. They can be practical, crisis-driven, transactional, and in come cases, even contentious. Always keep in mind that your following represents people who recognize the mutual value of their alignment with you in given circumstances. The best following is composed of people who operate with intelligence, principles, integrity, and a commitment to doing good work. It should include people with those characteristics from all levels and functions within your organization. Your following will be drawn from your connections and then from their connections. Your following becomes your "power base"—something we'll cover a bit later in this chapter.

What Is It That Attracts?

To attract a following, there needs to be something about who you are, what you're focused on, and how you conduct yourself that makes your followers believe that there is value to aligning with you. So, what is it about you that will attract others to you?

Everyone is in a position to attract a following. In order to get work done in most organizations, at the very least, we need people who are willing to work with us. At the simplest level your following is the one individual or group of individuals that you rely on to provide information, data, or support services needed to do your job. If your success vision is to grow in your business or your trade, you need a following of people who see and recognize the quality of your work, who recognize your potential, who trust you to perform effectively and with integrity in each new assignment, and who want to work with you.

There are many characteristics that can attract people to you professionally. Here's a partial list:

TRAITS THAT ATTRACT

Pleasant personality
Ability and willingness to listen
Sense of humor
Trustworthiness
Ability to clearly articulate issues
Willingness to collaborate
A commitment to producing good work
"Going the extra mile"
Business savvy
Commitment to the vision and mission of the organization
Ability to get things done
Inclusiveness
Personal humility
Intelligence and talent
Understanding of the business culture
Patience and perseverance
Successful track record

As you can see, it's who you are and what you are about that attracts. People will want to align with you when they feel connected to you on a person-to-person level. Just turn the scenario around and assess what it is that you seek from the people that you have *chosen* to align with. What is it about them that attracted you?

**Attracting a following does not mean
amassing a following. In many cases, less is more.**

Clearly, in the course of your work life you meet lots of people and develop positive working relationships with them. That's a good thing. Your following, however, is more intimate than just people who have heard about you. Your following are the people who have enough investment in what you are trying to achieve for the good of the organization to be "on call" when you need their help or support to advance an initiative or overcome an obstacle. These people are at every level of the organization.

Remember: attracting a following is not like going shopping. Your following is a by-product of what you do and how you conduct yourself. We never know the full extent or range of our following, but we can get a glimpse of it when we are looking for help. You don't need a "following" of hundreds—you just need to attract the right people. Be selective. Be both an attractor and follower yourself.

How Does the "Attracting" Process Work?

We are attracted to people who can make the right things happen. In most businesses, this means getting work done in a way that is satisfying, meaning-ful, and successful. We like to align ourselves with col-leagues, leaders, trades people and even customers who will bring the best out in us while producing outcomes that clearly help the organization succeed. Attracting a following doesn't mean that you are leading a follow-ing, although you may. It simply means that you have capabilities that are valuable to others who want to align with you.

You need to start by asking yourself what it is that you "bring to the party" that others value. Your knowl-edge, skills, and capabilities, either individually or together, are the assets that attract your following. There is an endless list of expertise that attracts. The chart below is one way of categorizing them:

EXPERTISE THAT ATTRACTS

Knowledge	Business Skills	Personal Capabilities
Process Flows	Negotiating	Written and oral
Legal Contracts	Systems	communication
Public Policy	Applications	Relationship
Statistical	Sales/Marketing	building
Methods	Financing/Auditing	Teamwork
Regulation	Research and	Innovation
Manufacturing	Analysis	Attention to detail
Investments	Implementing	Collaboration
Best Practices	Change	Problem-solving
Technology	Surveying	Out-of-the-box
Systems	Strategic Planning	thinking
Products/Services	Leadership	Truthfulness and
	Management/	integrity
	Supervision	Organization

Think of the kinds of information or help that people ask you for. That's where you'll find the seeds that are growing your following. The more expert you become in your areas of specialty or focus, the deeper and broader your following will become.

The key to your success lies in your ability to develop the range and depth of your knowledge, skills, and capabilities over time. Once again, it's about momentum. You can never let yourself stagnate. Attracting a following is an active move, not a passive one. So you've got to keep progressing. That means developing yourself, strengthening your brand by your actions, and demonstrating to your following that you are always on top of your game. Your following is counting on you to be at your best.

**The following you attract is the foundation
of your power base.**

The term "power base" is not the same as a "power broker" or "power trust." A power base is just that—a base or foundation of work allies (your following) that you can call on when you need support or assistance.

If you are in an organizational position of power, that doesn't mean you necessarily have a strong power base. You might think you do, but reality might be different. In organizations the real power you have is a function of what your following grants to you. The same people who can build you up can also cut you down.

Here's a true story of a high level manager whom we'll call Martin—a man who had advanced over a long career to a position reporting directly to the CEO. He had a highly influential job that impacted the way the company and its leaders were regarded by the public. Martin was a very talented man who understood his position of power in the company. The more license he had to influence decisions that supported his priorities for the company, the more demanding and unyielding he was with his colleagues and staff. He started to make unreasonable demands of people, became harshly critical, and gave direction that others considered improper or unwise. Many of the people who worked for him had been former peers who had helped him on his way up the organizational ladder. Many of the managers in other departments who had been well-served by him before his rise were disconcerted by his growing arrogance and single-mindedness.

While Martin was moving his agenda forward, he stopped nurturing his following. Worse than that, he began taking of advantage of them for his own purposes. Those who were supporters from his past, now his employees, felt betrayed, abused, and unvalued. Those from other departments who had once aligned with him felt that his view of the business did not represent a balanced perspective, threatening morale and performance.

So what, if any, negative effect did this have on Martin? Well, people started to talk about Martin to each other, to their friends, to managers in other departments, and to executives they knew. They talked about him in cubicles, elevators, corridors, restrooms, during meeting breaks, and at social events. From the lowest level of the organization to the highest, there were, at first, innocuous comments made in passing, that became more pointed. Some of them turned into branding statements like arrogant, unreasonable, and unfair. Everyone who had an issue with Martin had a following and those people had a following too. So little by little, during the course of about eighteen months, the whispers down the alley turned into blaring screams, seemingly heard by everyone except Martin. One day it was announced that Martin was no longer with the company. There was little surprise. He'd become a casualty of, among other things, a lost power base.

The Martin story illustrates the importance of your following. But it also demonstrates how important it is to serve those who are there for you. Attracting a following once isn't enough—you need to continue to earn their support by continuing to be worthy of it. It's a give and take relationship—it must be nurtured. You need to be willing to listen to and hear what the members of your following are telling you and what they need from you. This is not to say that you never disagree with the people who support you or that you always make popular decisions. Your following understands that you have responsibilities to the business and access to information that is different from theirs. They know that you may need to take action that may be controversial or disruptive. Anytime you have a role in implementing change, this will be the case. Your following just wants to understand the circumstances and the reasons behind your decisions and/or actions.

Your power base is not a monolith of people who suddenly show up en masse to bail you out of a fix. It's usually nearly impossible to truly understand the total composition of your power base. Sometimes there are people in it that you would never imagine—yes, there can be silent members, people who support you because, in a kind of obtuse way, you have helped them. You can sometimes be there for some of your following without your even knowing it. Your following, unless they are your direct reports, are generally a quiet populace that lies silently in the folds of your work life. But every now and then, when the need arises one or more of them surfaces to give you the help you need.

Here is the kind of help you might expect from your power base—or the kind of help you might be able to supply to those whom you follow:

An ear to the ground: Quiet rumblings often signal brewing issues or are precursors to conflicts. A phone call from someone in your power base can give you time to intervene.

A heads up on damaging comments: When your power base tells you about negative statements others are making about you or the work you are undertaking, you have a chance to do damage control.

Information in advance: Your power base is a strong source of advance information that you can use to kick start a project, change direction, better manage resources, or position yourself to make the right things happen. Any time you know something before it is made public, you have an advantage.

Specialized insights: Your power base can provide you with frontline knowledge that is often not in the line of sight of the leadership. This includes customer complaints, consumer attitudes, employee morale issues, labor-management relations, and regulator sensitivities. When you can articulate insights like these in a business context, your following has done both you and the business a real service.

Support and encouragement: There are times in business when the challenges you face are just plain hard. When you struggle, your power base can tell and one by one they will reach out to you, giving you the boost that you need to keep going.

I'll tell you one brief story about support and encouragement because it isn't often that CEOs get credit for caring enough to be part of the following of lower level managers. In my case, I'd been promoted to the position of Manager—Customer Support Services, which was a small department of staff professionals supporting a larger field organization. About two months after this move, there were major organizational changes at the top. Suddenly I was promoted to Director—Customer Service, now responsible for the centralization of the company's call center, overdue accounts receivable, and consumer programs. I was now in way over my head.

To make a long story short, the knowledge and accountability demands of this position were unbelievable. I worked and worked to try to bring myself up to speed when everything around me was chaotic. I was exhausted and it showed, but I had wonderful people around me who quite literally took care of me as best they could.

One gray winter day, I was called to a debriefing meeting of field employees who had issues with the way the call center operated during a storm-related power outage. The meeting was held in an old warehouse in the coal country of Pennsylvania. It was a dark and dreary place; the discussion was testy. While I was at the table, I got a message from the administrative staff that the CEO was on the phone and wanted to talk with me immediately. My stomach sank.

I marched up three flights of stairs into a vacant office and the call was put through. I heard the CEO's voice say, "Hi! Dawn. I know you have a lot going on right now. I just wanted to call and see how you were doing." I was awed by his caring. It was just the boost I needed to keep plugging.

Your power base—your wonderful following— reminds you, when you need it most, that you're not alone.

The Power of a Following

Each member of the "cast" we've been following gives us an interesting snapshot of the impact of a following in very different circumstances. Here's a look at how each player managed his or her following:

Matt Clinger—Matt represents the classic case of a manager who was only interested in attracting a following "up" the organization. He demonstrated little if any interest in developing relationships with "lower level" employees—those below his rank—and often appeared to hold them in low regard. Matt was a poor listener who, in most meetings, dominated discussion with his own views. At times he followed people around to "check" on them, creating the perception that he didn't trust his employees. None of these behaviors enabled Matt to attract a diverse following. As a result, he had no power base to speak of, and once his executive pals were out of power, so was he.

Hal Dodger—Hal wanted to do everything on his own, so he set himself up as a lone wolf. He didn't work effectively with others and didn't want them to be part of his work. Instead of attracting a following, he repelled it. His relationships were poor with his colleagues and internal customers. Consequently, as his performance declined, no one tipped him off about what was being said about him and no one offered support. His decline and eventual dismissal were the dismal outcomes of, among other things, no following.

Cliff Black—Cliff built a strong following that provided him with a flawless power base while he was plant manager. When he became vice president of the district office, he left his power base behind. Not only did he have no following in his new job, he didn't seem to be able to attract one. His plant following was confined to a single location, so he had nothing to draw from when he moved on. As a result, Cliff was isolated in his new position, having no support system within reach. Without a following, he was unable to lead effectively.

Julia Masters—Julia's following among key managers was a by-product of her commitment to her professional growth. The people she worked for were impressed and inspired by her dedication to her schooling and her ability to quickly transfer knowledge and skills to the workplace. Yes, good work attracts attention especially when it is done to serve the interests of the company, not oneself. As Julia's management roles expanded, she struggled initially to earn the respect and support of some senior direct reports. Her knowledge and courage to do the right things to position them for success ultimately created a strong followership. It took time, effort, and selflessness to gain it.

Dr. Barker—Weaknesses in administrative processes and policies that had escalated as Dr. Barker's practice grew caused deterioration of morale. The support of the office manager and staff, his longtime following, had become dangerously eroded. His quick decision to fix what was broken in the practice restored the faith and strength of his internal following in time to avoid any negative effect on his client base—his other powerful following. Dr. Barker's situation demonstrates how forgiving your following can be when you take action to make things right.

Bert and Lee Cook—The Cook's attracted a following, built on it, and never looked back. The success of their restaurant venture is a classic example of the power of the following. The students they taught, the parents of those students, friends and associates in all aspects of their lives were attracted by their energy, creativity, courage, quality food and service, and their joy in entertaining. In the restaurant business, you can never please everyone. The longevity of their business is testimony to the quality of their power base, which translated into a loyal customer base.

Doug Hart—Here's a great example of attracting a following from the ground up. Doug started out in administrative work in a hospital and took it upon himself to develop relationships with cardiologists. These doctors saw something in him. When he expressed an interest in learning more, they had enough shared interest in him to teach him. His growing knowledge and operating room skills expanded the depth and quality of his following, which expanded to outside firms selling heart care technology. When he left the hospital to work in sales, he simply expanded his following, never letting go of those positive relationships that were part of his hospital experiences.

In a Nutshell

Your private moves prepare you for your public moves. To attract a following, you move from staying connected to engaging the support, interest, and talent of people who recognize your unique capabilities. Your personal brand comes from your knowledge, skills, and attributes, and it can be enhanced or diminished by your following.

As you grow your following, you deepen and broaden the base of support you need to achieve success. Your following consists of dynamic relationships that are fundamentally unstructured. It is at times composed of people with whom we are connected organizationally; we are expected to support and be supported by them. But we all move on, so the people we leave behind are always in a position to remain part of our following by virtue of what we represent. Other times our following comes from a series of loose associations—people we meet casually to exchange views, project team members, individuals from the community, and even customers.

Attracting a following is an ongoing requirement of business fitness. The more diverse our following, the more significant our power base becomes. Our power base has the potential to liberate us, to give us strength and courage, to enable us to turn grand ideas into reality, and to provide us with an important sense of belonging. To be business fit is to have a strong foundation of relationships that are aligned with the kind of success we seek.

Attracting a following brings with it the obligation to be worthy of the support you're being given. That means remembering to nurture your following with your own support when circumstances warrant. Remember the adage: As you sow, so shall you reap.

The inevitable expectation of your following is that, when the time is right, you will take the lead. You need to be prepared and be ready for that—your next public move.

PUBLIC MOVES INVENTORY: ATTRACT A FOLLOWING

The first public move is to attract a following, building support from people at all levels of the organization that enable you to utilize your capabilities effectively to produce quality work for the good of the business. Use your answers to identify your brand and the people in your organization that make up or need to make up your following. Then develop a plan to increase, improve, or develop the relationships that will be mutually beneficial.

1. Describe the way *you* see your brand identity in the categories below:

Appearance/ Style	Knowledge/ Skills	Personal Capabilities

2. Ask each of the following to describe the way *they* see your brand in each category.

	Appearance/ Style	Knowledge/ Skills	Personal Capabilities
Boss			
Peers			
Employees			
Customers			

3. List five people from your power base in each category shown. Describe what actions you need to take to reinforce your relationships.

Frontline Workers	Supervisors/ Managers	Executives	Actions
1.			
2.			
3.			
4.			
5.			

Chapter 9

TAKE THE LEAD

Provide direction and create momentum

This is your moment! Let the games begin!

Taking the lead is about accepting accountability for the work produced by others, the ultimate measure of your business fitness. When you have the lead, you are in the public eye of your following and all those who have a stake in what is achieved under your direction. It doesn't matter whether you're leading a company, a work group, a team, or a meeting: When you have the lead, you are the one responsible for the work and accountable for the outcome. There is no room for excuses and no mistaking where the buck stops.

Taking the lead is a choice. If the lead isn't something you want, don't take it.

The essence of business fitness is maximizing your opportunities to choose. When you are prepared and ready to move your work life forward, you have a strong foundation for choice. When your choices fit your success model, they will likely take you where you want to go.

There is a difference between "taking" the lead and "getting"or "accepting" the lead. "Getting" the lead is when you find yourself in a leadership position by default. You somehow get maneuvered into the position. You don't choose or reject the role—it just happens to you. "Accepting" the lead is reactive and can be two-pronged. Someone in a position of power asks you to take on a leadership responsibility or your "following" appeals to you to assume the role and you say, "yes," without fully understanding or clarifying the expectations.

"Taking" the lead is done on your terms—you may choose to take it when someone in a position of power offers it or your "following" makes it clear that they want you in that role. You may also choose to decline if the actual or potential risks are beyond your tolerance. The key is to understand what the "lead" means in each circumstance and how it will enable you to utilize your capabilities, perform work you believe has real value, and move your career forward.

Sometimes the lead may look very tempting on the surface. It may appear to come with personal benefits: visibility, authority, access to influential people, and privileges. In this case, remember the adage: "You don't get something for nothing." Generally, the greater the perceived benefits of the lead, the higher the performance expectations. You need to know realistically what you are getting into and not be lured by what may be the glitz. So check yourself: Be sure you are taking the lead so you can produce an outcome that fits your capabilities, interests, and standards. If taking the lead becomes tantamount to self-torture because the role isn't compatible with your capabilities and needs, then those benefits won't be so sweet. The best situation is when you can take the lead by stepping forward at the right time and offering your services. That can mean volunteering to run a project, chairing a committee, or being the preferred candidate for a leadership job.

Warning:
Be certain that the lead you take is the lead you want. If you're any good, you'll likely have the lead for a long time.

Taking the lead means getting in the right game at the right time and playing to win. Here's the challenge—defining what "right" means. As you increase your business fitness through your private and public moves, you increase your ability to read the tea leaves where you work. You start to get a sense of the kinds of leadership assignments that are the right fit for you. The key is not to get too impatient about taking the lead. It is always better to wait for the right opportunity than to jump on the first one.

Part of your preparation for taking the lead is demonstrating to your management and your following what your business "passions" are. Take advantage of opportunities to share your views on business: ways to improve customer service, new product or service concepts, process improvements, communications and performance effectiveness. Demonstrate that you have developed technical, process, and/or management expertise to ensure that work is completed as required. Your willingness to take on new assignments and complete them well and on time showcases your commitments to the business. What you know and do within and above your job responsibilities position you for the kind of opportunities that will fit you best when you step forward or are asked to take the lead.

Taking the lead involves accountability and includes a degree of risk. When you are in a leadership situation, you provide the direction that others follow to achieve the expected outcome. If they don't succeed, you don't succeed. We all want to make choices that result in success, so it is important not to be naïve when taking the lead. First, you need to determine the risk by weighing the odds for success. So ask yourself what the chances are for a successful outcome. Is it:
1. A sure thing
2. Risky
3. Unlikely

In order to answer this question you need to understand clearly some key things:

1. What is the scope of the task? How big is it?
2. To whom are you accountable?
3. What are the expected outcomes and/or
   deliverables?
4. How much decision-making authority do you
   have?
5. What resources will you be given (dollars,
   people, time)?
6. What are the deadlines?
7. What would be your ongoing involvement if
   the effort is successful?

Then ask yourself whether or not you want to take the
lead and the risk. Remember: The clarity of *your* direction and the capability of the people you are leading
are the key elements of success. If you don't think the
people you will be leading can do the job, then your
chances of succeeding are low. So look long and hard at
your people resources—their capabilities, commitment, and work ethic. As you can see, there's a lot to
weigh before you take the lead.

  Sometimes you'll be "assigned" the lead whether
you want it or not. That's just the reality of organizations. The more business fit you are, the more equipped
you will be to make the best out of what you might consider a less than perfect situation. Even if the lead is
imposed on you, the first step you take is to get as much
clarity as you can about what is expected. In some situations you may find yourself in a position to influence the

scope of the leadership assignment you've been given. That's a good thing because it demonstrates your ability to see a "better way" and positions you to reconfigure the effort to fit the capabilities of your team.

I'm a big fan of "scoping documents" or "charters" for leadership assignments that are not job positions. These are helpful when you are given a special project or temporary assignment requiring your leadership. These documents put the parameters of the assignment in writing—clarifying expectations, time frames, resources, and the like. Most of the time, you will need to write this document yourself and discuss it with your management. That's just the way it is in most organizations, and it gives you the opportunity to influence the direction of your assignment—something that good leaders want to do.

After you have drafted your "charter," present it to your management as the first step in your planning and organizing process. Explain that clarification of direction, accountabilities, and expectations is essential to the effectiveness of your team. The charter helps you control "scope creep" and changes in expectations by both management and your team. Use it like an informal contract to keep all the stakeholders in your effort on the same page. If your management wants to change the project scope, that's fine, but, as the leader, you will be able to use the charter to renegotiate the resources and time frame needed to achieve the expected outcomes. When you take the lead, your followers expect you to protect the integrity of the effort and minimize or remove obstacles to their work. The charter positions you to do that.

The Likely, the Risky, and the Unlikely

Weighing the success potential for any leadership opportunity is more art than science. At the very least, before you take the lead, give some thought to what your chances are for a win.

I've had a few of these leadership opportunities of my own. The three that I share below illustrate how the process can work.

1) **The Likely:** I was assigned the leadership of a consumer program that the state mandated for all the energy companies it regulated. This effort required a massive communications effort to over a million customers, using all forms of media and grassroots initiatives, over a five-year period. To take the lead meant to ensure that the messages were delivered appropriately and accurately within a fully expended budget. On another level, the lead meant influencing cross-industry and regulator decisions about the content of those messages and their presentation, so that consumers would understand the information and be able to act effectively on it. What a concept!

To be successful, I needed to provide clear direction to my staff who handled the details and to my industry colleagues and professional partners who were driving the material development. The overarching structure, regulator oversight, collaboration by all parties, and momentum of the program resulted in a notable success.

2) **The Risky:** The company that I was working for had developed a collaborative agreement with the labor union to implement a continuous improvement

program to improve labor-management relations, increase employee involvement in decision making, and enhance understanding of company operations and challenges. I was selected for one of the "special project" manager positions—my "constituency" was frontline field and office employees. This role required efforts to build trust with labor leaders who were teamed with me and then to provide opportunities for them to be heard by executive management.

There were many obstacles to overcome on both sides: old scars, new doubts, gaps in understanding about the business, personality differences, and struggles with team decision making. My prior experience working with labor leaders was zero. My firsthand knowledge of labor issues, contracts, and grievances was about to increase a thousandfold. The road was rough although on some level there was growth and newfound friendships. The initiative was not sustained because its structure was awkward and inefficient; trust issues abounded. Even when there were signs of progress, no one ever used the word "success;" in the end, most considered it a failure. The effort simply faded away.

3) **The Unlikely:** Sometimes you're just doomed before you start—you can't escape the lead and you can't pull off a success. This happened to me. One of the company's operations VPs was given an assignment by the CEO to complete a follow-up employee opinion survey. Surveys were not his "thing" but he had no way out of the assignment. Because of my employee involvement experiences, the VP was given the green light to assign the leadership of this task to me. I knew that the VP did not have his heart in this. I suspected that this

would be a matter of "going through the motions" and that no action would be taken on the basis of the findings. At the same time, I knew that the methodology used to gather this data and the presentation of the findings would be well-scrutinized by the senior executives to whom it would be presented.

I wrote a charter and had it approved by the VP. Then I went to my following, asked for help from those with the right capabilities, great senses of humor, and a realistic expectation of what we were doing. My assessment of the task was correct—the deliverable was exactly what the VP wanted, the presentation went off like clockwork, and none of the recommendations ever saw the light of day. The project team had a blast working together. We taught each other aspects of survey techniques and statistical analyses that we didn't know before, and we distinguished ourselves as a group for a product well-constructed. Then, with a sardonic bit of laughter, we just moved on.

Preparing to Take the Lead

Much of preparing to take the lead starts with your private moves. You have to stay well because the lead takes both mental and physical energy. The lead may seem like it's about you when in fact it's about everyone else. You need to have the energy to get in tune with the expectations of all the players—the individual who has given you the lead, the people who are following, and those who will be affected by the results you produce.

You also need to stay focused. The root of your business fitness is in the focus you maintain on your success goals. Your success as a leader is about your focus on the goals of the group and/or the work that you are accountable for. You must be crystal clear about what your goals are as the leader or your followers will become confused, frustrated, or de-energized. Here is something important to remember:

**Leaders define reality, set direction,
and anticipate the future.**

That may sound pretty heavy-duty, but think about it. If a leader doesn't give you a clear sense of how the business is performing—the team, the department, or the profit center—and what the likelihood is that the business is positioned for success, then you, as a follower, are going to work every day with blinders on. Unfortunately, that's what happens too often. Leaders aren't clearly tuned into the very reality that they need to be defining so that you and I can do the work and respond to the challenges that will ensure that the business and we are successful.

When you take the lead, you need to showcase your commitment, energy, motivation, and *courage*. Think about it: It takes courage to state the truth about the realities in your organization. It doesn't matter if you are the business owner, a senior executive, a department manager, a front line supervisor, or a co-worker. You need to understand the realities of your work, your work group, your business, and your industry. That's part of what you do when you stay current and why you stay connected with people who have perspectives that shed light on reality.

Business realities are many things. Here are a few:

- Financial performance—Is the business making money?
- Budget management—Are you doing quality work at the least cost?
- Productivity—Are employees committed to completing as much work as they can daily?
- Employee capabilities and potential—Are employees increasing their skills?
- Competition—How does the business compare to its competitors?
- Marketplace—What are the risks and trends that could affect the business in the future?
- Technology—Is the hardware and software effective and reliable?
- Salaries and Benefits—Can the business afford rising employee costs? Can it attract and retain talented people?

It takes courage for leaders to talk about these realities. And please don't think this just pertains to high-level realities. Each of these translates to the smallest work group and project team. Every subset of an organization has performance requirements and should have goals and plans to achieve them. This means that, at every level, there are questions about resources expended to get work done, the performance quality of contributors, the implications of outcomes, and the credibility of data. There are realities associated with every range, scope, and level of leadership—and good leaders define them, develop strategies to address them, and implement actions to overcome them. The best way to prepare for taking the lead are your private moves:

- Stay well
- Stay focused
- Stay current
- Stay connected

Leadership takes practice.
Take small steps before making your big move.

I can recall dozens of conversations with employees eager for management or supervisory positions who routinely fail to be selected for them. Almost to a person, they are told that they did not get the job because they lacked leadership experience. Their comeback was, "How am I supposed to get leadership experience if I'm never selected for a job supervising others?" The answer is that there are many ways to demonstrate your preparation for leadership jobs that aren't jobs.

If you're in the habit of staying connected, you're developing a broad base of relationships within and outside your organization. I'm sure you can make a long list of outside leadership roles that you can choose: coaching community sports teams, heading up committees where you worship, participating on non-profit boards, being a scout leader, or organizing a community function. People see you in these roles and find out how you performed. Once again, it's who knows you. Your public reputation follows you wherever you go, including back to work.

On the job you develop significant work-related expertise—technical, managerial, administrative, and interpersonal. Take advantage of opportunities to mentor individuals and groups, orient new employees, and volunteer to conduct training. Each of these aligns you with components of the leadership profile and people will see and/or hear about how you performed. When your organization needs someone to temporarily fill in for someone on extended leave or in an "acting" position, that may be another place for you to showcase how you lead. Your following will help you spot these opportunities and will likely help you when you land one.

Part of your preparation to take the lead is to be a continuous observer of the notable leaders in your organization. Think about asking one of those leaders to mentor you for a set period of time—say, three months. Read books on leadership and about great leaders from all walks of life: business, government, science, social reform, education, exploration—anything that interests you. This is part of staying current and a precursor to taking the lead.

As you prepare to take the lead, spend some time thinking realistically about the kind of lead that suits you. Remember: business fitness is about achieving the kind of success you want—not what you think you can get, what others might want for you, or what might fall into your lap. It's about exercising choice to create the life you want.

There are all kinds of business leadership roles, not just the highest levels that you see characterized on TV or written about in the *Wall Street Journal.* When you lead, your followers grant you the license to take them somewhere that will, in the end, feel worthwhile. So think about what kind and level of leadership you wish to pursue, recognizing that as your experience and successes grow, you may choose to expand you horizons. Here is a starter list of leadership positions that you can add to:

- Business Owner
- Executive
- Department Head
- Manager/Supervisor
- Project Manager
- Special Projects Leader
- Dean/Superintendent/Principal
- Account Executive
- Executive Director
- Team Leader

These are formal leadership roles with a wide berth of responsibilities and potential impacts on the organization. They put you in a position publicly to be accountable for specific goals and outcomes that have been assigned to you and your specific team of followers.

There are situations where you can take the lead that are less formalized while giving you important opportunities to impact the organization. Here are two of them:

- Subject Matter Expert
- Communicator

Since the primary role of leaders is to define reality, then people who manage and/or control information and knowledge are in a position to take the lead in a very targeted way.

Imagine that you are a subject matter expert on telephony, legal precedents, or retail market trends in an organization that is failing because of problems in any one of these areas. You are called to a meeting by an executive who has little or no knowledge in your area but is poised to make key decisions that will affect the organization's profitability and/or reputation. Her decision will be made on the basis of the information you provide. At that meeting, which may involve top people in your organization, you will have the lead by virtue of what you know, how you apply it to the organization's issues, and how you communicate it. In this very public forum, you will have the lead, albeit for a snapshot in time and with a temporary following. You will likely be called back to talk with this group again and be asked to provide data and materials.

This leadership situation is quite different from leading a team. It is what you know and what others will do with what you share that puts you in this unique position to lead. You will be held accountable for the accuracy and credibility of your knowledge and information while the executive group will be accountable for the decisions made on the basis of what they heard from you. The better your contribution to this process, the more likely it will be that you are called upon again as a subject matter expert. This kind of leadership can have significant success rewards in the right organization, or it can provide you with the kinds of expert credentials that will create career mobility. Once again, it becomes a matter of choice.

Here's another scenario: If you've heard it once, you've heard it a thousand times: Communication is what makes or breaks an organization. When communication is good or when it is poor, it affects employee morale, shareholder confidence, customer satisfaction, product appeal, regulator confidence, and public image. Effective communication is about sending clear and appropriate messages to the right audiences at the right time.

The problem is that, in most organizations, there is low clarity about what leaders want to say to their constituencies. Complex issues need to be sorted out and explained in straightforward terms. That means that the organization's leadership must share a common understanding of those messages and how to handle them. When the leadership team can't seem to come to a common understanding, all too often they simply leave the communications issues unresolved or worse, they go ahead and communicate their own individual messages. Poor communications delivery and unmanaged messages can break the back of an organization.

Now, imagine that you have one of two possible roles in your organization: communications specialist or meeting scribe (a fancy word for the person assigned to take notes). I'm sure you've been at meetings where the leader asks for a volunteer to record the meeting's proceedings. In unison everyone takes a slug of coffee or a donut bite, avoiding eye contact. However, if the ideas to be discussed or the decisions to be made at the meeting are significant, the person taking the notes will exercise the lead in a unique way.

The person taking notes or designated to put together formal communications about the meeting outcome is positioned to influence the direction, tone, and language of the message. The discussion will surely be diverse and, in some cases, politically driven. There will be all manner of interests that will need to be incorporated into a final position that everyone can accept. Most meeting leaders have difficulty bringing closure around the message because they are more engaged in managing the dynamics of the personalities than in synthesizing the myriad of ideas and positions. The person writing the proceedings is focused on capturing the common ground of thinking and framing it into a coherent message.

Anyone who can turn discussion points into direction through the synthesis of meaning, intent, and context has achieved a unique leadership position. Just like the subject matter expert, this position is more situational than organizational. When your brand includes this skill, you will likely be asked to sit at the table where important organizational issues are discussed and resolved. In time you will develop insights into the business that are deep and broad until you become a kind of subject matter expert on strategic and tactical matters that impact the organization. In the course of things, you will expand your following and may very well find yourself being asked to take the lead in a more sustained public way. It's your choice.

Leaders assess risk and remove obstacles.

Before you take the lead, you need to know what you are getting yourself and your followers into. You start by making sure that you have a realistic view of your skills. It's not enough to "think" you can lead; you have to "know" that you have the skills to lead effectively. Your following will help you assess yourself once you have a clear understanding of what the scope of responsibilities and expectations are of having the lead.

Most of the time we become so flattered that we are being considered for the lead that we forget to ask what is required. It's a big mistake to believe that the person positioned to give you the lead really knows whether you have all the capabilities required to be successful. All too often the requirements of leadership responsibilities are not thought through beforehand, another reason to draft that charter. In the course of events, the requirements of the lead may change with expectations being added that don't align with your interests or skills. The politics of the organization can play a huge part in your ability to be effective in the lead, so you need to understand who all the players are that can influence the direction of your lead.

Your following will be as affected by the quality of your risk management on the front end of your leadership as you are. If you don't have enough clout to go along with your lead, then you will be helpless to remove the inevitable obstacles that can block the work progress of your following. If you can't remove obstacles, you can't sustain the motivation of your team. You'll risk losing your sense of worth and compromise the success of your efforts. It is critical to complete your leadership "due diligence" before you take the lead and then negotiate the conditions you need to achieve a positive outcome.

Become the Leader that You Want to Be

Successful leaders come in all types, and I'm sure that you have a few in mind. Here are a few leadership traits that I believe are essential to your business fitness:

- Clear direction
- Commitment to the work
- Personal responsibility and accountability
- Ongoing, quality communication
- Support for the following
- Clear performance standards
- Personal ethics and integrity
- Decisiveness
- Change management capability
- Balanced perspective
- Sense of humor

The sum total of your business fitness is reflected in your leadership.

Every success you achieve when you take the lead increases the value of your personal business currency. The more effective you are when you lead, the more your success momentum will grow.

Business fitness is like any form of fitness: The stronger and more capable you become, the more challenges you can take on. If you're a golfer and shoot below par consistently on a public course, then you'll consider playing on a tougher course or in a tournament. If you train hard and run in a 3K race, you may choose to test yourself at 5K. If you have a personal trainer, the stronger you get, the more he or she will increase the difficulty of the exercises. In each case you can decline and say, "That's as far as I want to go" because I've achieved what I set out to do. But if you want to move forward, you'll continue to take on new challenges until you've reached the level of success you want.

The Cast: Leads Taken and Leads Lost

Three of the cases we've been following demonstrate how taking the lead can play out.

Dr. Barker owned his veterinary practice, so it was clear that he was the organizational leader. He made the rules, created the culture, amassed a following among staff and clients, and made decisions based on his assessment of priorities, needs, and urgency. Since Dr. Barker was both business owner and practicing veterinarian, his perception of himself as the leader was an outgrowth of his experiences in the exam room with clients. Although he fully appreciated the contributions of his staff, he perceived that their leader was the office manager. In truth, the office manager saw him as the leader and herself as his agent. So when she was unable to resolve staff problems, she needed Dr. Barker to remove obstacles and make business decisions on "back office" matters based on her recommendations. As soon as Dr. Barker understood that his leadership was needed to enhance the office manager's leadership, a whole host of problems were resolved.

Cliff Black accepted the lead because it was given to him—dangled like a shiny lure to a hungry fish. He already had the lead in the perfect environment—one that aligned his experience, training, and personal needs with the requirements of the plant. When the vice president's job at the district office came his way, he took it without essential risk assessment because the "giver" thought he was right for the job. We can all appreciate how flattered Cliff must have felt by the offer and why he would have felt optimistic about his prospects.

Unfortunately, Cliff wasn't prepared for the change in culture, the leadership expectations, and the scope of work of his new job. He may have thought he was ready to be a vice president in that setting, but he was not prepared to do it successfully.

Doug Hart demonstrated how becoming a subject matter expert can get you the lead. Because of Doug's insatiable desire to learn everything he could about cardiac catheterization procedures, he built up both subject matter knowledge and applications skills working with doctors in the OR. The more he learned and the more capable he became as a trusted technical colleague, the more his personal value grew. When he moved from the hospital to medical equipment sales, his new role was essentially entrepreneurial. Doug had a territory and a large contingent of doctors that he served both by providing excellent products but also by providing insightful knowledge grounded in personal experience. He became a knowledge leader and a successful sales professional.

In a Nutshell

Whether you are an entrepreneur, corporate or organizational executive, manager, or professional, your success depends upon your ability to take the lead at the right time. Your following is counting on you to pick your best spots, ensure that you understand what is expected, and position yourself with the kind of authority that will maximize their ability to perform effectively.

Taking the lead is a public move so it will attract attention to your ability to produce results and be accountable for what your following delivers. Preparation for the lead means learning and practicing leadership skills, developing a clear understanding of the realities of the business, and assessing the risks for success. Your performance as a leader will position you for additional leadership opportunities, so you need to be sure that the leads you take are the leads you want. Once you have the lead, if you are any good, you will likely have it for a while.

The lead can be a permanent position in the organization, a project assignment, or a specialized role, so choose leadership opportunities that fit the success path you are pursuing. Your business fitness will be showcased when you lead. That's the excitement of this public move.

PUBLIC MOVES INVENTORY: TAKE THE LEAD

The second public move is to take the lead, using your business fitness capabilities to deliver positive results to your organization. You need to be prepared to take the lead, which means taking stock of your leadership skills and aligning them to the needs of your organization. Use your responses here to develop your leadership plan.

List 3 of your strongest leadership skills? How are you using them? How do you want to use them?

Leadership Skill	Current Use	Desired Use
1.		
2.		
3.		

List 3 leadership skills you need to strengthen. What will you do to improve them?

Leadership Skill	Steps to Improve
1.	
2.	
3.	

List 3 situations where you have taken the lead. What was the outcome? What could you have done to improve it?

Situation	Outcome	Improvement Steps
1.		
2.		
3.		

Describe a situation where you currently seek a leadership role? What is your plan?

Situation **Action Plan**

Chapter 10

IMPLEMENT NEW IDEAS

Use innovation to fuel your business and your career

It all comes down to this—when you're business fit, you see the big picture more clearly. Ideas for breaking new ground and solving problems are in your line of sight. You're ready to make things happen that will make a lasting difference. It's time to put your game face on and make another public move.

Whether we like it or not, we work in a "what have you done for me lately" world. Ultimately, that's what business competition is all about—the ability to take new steps forward to attract and retain customers—your organization's external following and the source of its profitability. The lifeblood of any business is its ability to turn new ideas into practice ahead of the pack. In business, when there is no innovation, there is no growth. Once the growth stops, decay sets in and the rest is simply not very pretty.

Your ability to innovate new ideas and then implement them is a huge asset for your personal brand, a major attractor for your following, your ticket to finding the right lead to take, and the springboard for ongoing career success.

To put this in perspective, imagine what you would be doing now to make a living if you never implemented a new idea. It is likely that you would be in the career you announced to your relatives at your fifth birthday party. Clearly, I would be an unemployed sharpshooter from a defunct traveling circus. Think of all the kids today, some of whom could be related to you, who say they want to be professional skateboarders or bass guitar players in a rock band, doctors or graphic artists, forensic scientists or fashion models. Some may turn their idea into a real career and most will not—perhaps to your delight. Most of the time, we trade our childhood fantasies (ideas) for dreams or goals that we can turn into successful careers. Cultivating new ideas is vital to our own growth; implementing these new ideas at the right time and in the right place is the keystone for our success.

Business growth and prosperity are built on innovation—the act of introducing something new. Your personal success capital is increased when you are perceived as a practical innovator. That means your ideas seem doable, affordable, and timely. They are connected to business priorities and have success potential. When you spew out ideas willy-nilly, you will more than likely be viewed as a "loose cannon" and your ideas deemed suspect—even your good ideas. So it is critical to develop your ideas and then apply strategic thinking to determine the right time, venue, and approach for offering them.

When ideas never see the light of day in a business, it's usually because management can't see how they can be practically implemented. So you must articulate your ideas in terms of the need that they will address and the organization's ability to use existing resources and infrastructure to make them happen.

"Bad" ideas can become "great" ideas when the time is right. Patience is your idea's greatest advantage.

Implementing new ideas is where all your business fitness comes together. When you stay current on what's going on in the business environment, you understand and see what the trends and needs are. By staying connected, you've engaged in discussions with informed people on those trends and the "political" conditions of your business environment—so you know what the obstacles will be when it's time to implement your idea. Your following is positioned to turn your idea into practice when the time is right, responding to your lead when it has been established.

The struggle around implementing new ideas comes from the people in your organization who may not endorse them, feel threatened by them, only support their own ideas, or generally resist change. Often, you will have most, if not all, of these obstacles to deal with concurrently. And because resistance can be daunting, many people give up. Now, there is a difference between giving up, which to me means total abandonment, and deferring action. After all, resistance isn't always at the same level all of the time. This is where patience and hard work come into play.

If you really believe your idea will improve your organization, and its stakeholders—investors, allies, the community, employees and you—then you will feel compelled to keep your idea alive. That means you will continue to use your connections, your following, and your leadership opportunities to reinforce the insights that you have developed to influence thinking within your organization.

**Support from one key person
can turn a "dead" idea into a "live" one.**

Throughout history there are many examples of how a talented, struggling artist, like Shakespeare or Michelangelo, rises to greatness once discovered and funded by a patron. Arts patrons are regarded by their community or society as supremely knowledgeable about what constitutes great work; if they say the work of an artist is great, then the populace sees it as great too.

It's pretty much the same way in business. If you have a great idea for how to improve the appeal of a product, the efficiency of a work process, the capabilities of new software, a fairer discipline policy, or a more profitable pricing system, that idea will likely develop traction if and when you find yourself a "patron"—a respected leader with a track record for implementing new ideas and the resources to make them happen. So what does that tell you: That you need to use your connections and your following to identify the prospective "patron" who will help you get your idea implemented.

Finding a "patron" also takes patience. It is a step-by-step process where you try your idea out in small bits on others before you present it to the person who can help it take off. Always keep in mind that a raw idea always needs a reality check. As you informally share it with others from your following, you'll discover issues and angles that need to be clarified and the right words to trigger positive reactions. By testing your idea with others, you keep your finger on the pulse of the organization

---

The value of a new idea is measured by the results it is expected to deliver.

You must be crystal clear about how your idea will make your organization better, stronger, and more profitable. It's like anything else in business: You have to have a strong value proposition and a tight business case, establishing how the organization will benefit by investing time and money to implement your idea. There's always a lot more to implementing an idea in practice than there appears on the surface. If you ignore those implications, your following will lose confidence in you and be reluctant to support the initiative. So it has to be clear that the "pain" associated with implementing your new idea will be worth it.

Implementing a new idea creates change.
People don't like change. Now what?

It doesn't matter how great your idea is or how promising its outcome. It doesn't matter if it is a big idea or a small one. It doesn't matter if it comes about in a small business, a nonprofit agency, a work unit, or a big company. Your idea changes something. It may replace the way work has been done, improve the performance of your product, reduce the price to consumers, provide an opportunity to earn a bonus, or enhance the quality of data. No matter what your idea offers, it puts an end to something.

It is common for an organization's management to announce proudly an "improvement"—its new idea for the way something should be done. You might be told how the new compensation system will position you to achieve a higher pay increase by meeting stretch goals. You might be told how new computer software will help you to process more customer calls or generate more real time data for analysis. You might be told how a modification to a product or service will make it more appealing and easier for you to sell. These are the promises of innovation—new ideas designed to improve business performance.

These promises always sound great because achieving them as described would have value for the organization, but there are always issues. These issues are not usually a function of the validity of the idea but of the organization's ability to implement it. If you can't turn your idea into practice in a way that delivers the benefits, the idea will be a failure.

Turning ideas into practice requires the willingness and capabilities of others to *end* the way they have done things in order to accommodate the requirements of the innovation. That means they have to trade what they have been comfortable and successful doing for something they may be uncomfortable doing with no guarantees of personal success.

Change disrupts our patterns, makes us feel off balance, and spawns resistance.

There are lots of reasons why we resist change, particularly around innovation. The center of it is the unknown. For some reason there's a tendency to think that change means things will get worse. So even if we have a boss no one can stand, when a new boss gets assigned to us, we're still uneasy.

It is classic for resistance to occur when organizations automate a work process to increase efficiency. Employees (hopefully) are trained on how to execute the new technology and are then expected to apply the training. Too often, employees don't "trust the computer" to perform the new functions correctly. This is a change from the way they used to do things— a way that always seemed to worked reliably before. These folks don't want to end up making mistakes because of the technology. So to protect themselves, they keep pencil and paper backup documents to check the computer's calculations and/or data storage accuracy. When this happens, the benefits of the new idea cannot be realized.

Here are a few reasons why some new ideas mean change:

- New levels of performance may be required
- Expected outcomes seem more challenging
- New knowledge and skills are needed
- Work involves relationships with new people
- New processes and/or procedures are established

Each one of these changes means that people need to perform differently. It doesn't matter if the change is large or small, the potential for resistance is the same.

Managing change is as much art as it is science. Part of your business fitness regimen for staying current and taking the lead should be expanding your knowledge of successful techniques for managing change. Communication is the key to preparing the people in your organization for the implementation of a new idea. A meeting announcement or broadcast e-mail isn't enough. A new idea that creates change requires *relentless* communication about the context, need, and value of the change.

This communication must be brutally honest (no sugarcoating allowed!) about the reasons why this idea needs to be implemented now, about who is accountable for the results, and about how it will be implemented, tracked, and adjusted when conditions warrant. People need to know the kind and frequency of information they will get about the progress of change, including how it is matching expectations. Supervision needs to provide lots of direct support for employees striving to meet the new performance expectations. When you communicate these commitments up front and deliver on your promises, you will minimize resistance.

In spite of all the good intentions inherent in your new idea, you will have some critical mass of people at all levels of your organization resisting change. Some people will overtly resist by creating "noise," push-back, or nonparticipation. Others will covertly resist by "waiting it out," expecting the leadership to tire of the resistance and abandon the idea. If you have the lead, and hopefully you do, for implementation of your idea, you will need to step up and handle that resistance. This is no simple or pleasant task, and although there has been a lot of important work written on this topic, here are some very simple "do's" and "don'ts" for dealing with resistance:

DO

- Stay the course
- Reiterate the value of the innovation, the purpose of the change, and the benefits
- Listen to and act on constructive feedback
- Listen to resistance and reinforce the organization's direction
- Ask people what help they need in order to adjust to new requirements
- Provide training directly related to goal achievement
- Provide ongoing communication about performance against expectations

DON'T

- Own the resistance of others; their resistance is their issue
- Reward resistance by softening requirements
- Tolerate behavior that interferes with the performance of others
- Abandon the initiative because of it

It is not necessary for people to buy into the change. They simply have to perform as expected.

A successfully implemented new idea results from the collective efforts of employees, management, and/or work partners. This is true whether you work with only one other person or many. When the change is successfully implemented, the resisters and the non-resisters will own the outcome because it came from their collective efforts. Buy-in is a by-product of successfully managed change.

Implementing new ideas requires up-front support from your following, a well-crafted and clearly communicated plan, strong monitoring of progress, and recognition of the contributions of everyone along the way, especially those on the frontline of the change. By the time your idea is implemented, you will have shared the credit for both the idea and the implementation with many others. If you try to hoard the credit, you will dim perceptions of your brand. Success in business is a shared experience. The more credit you give away, the more esteem you will accrue.

The Mysterious Sources of New Ideas

The question often asked is, "Where do I find these new ideas?" I've heard it said, "There are no new ideas." In business most new ideas are a synthesis of existing ideas, a kind of reconfiguring, realigning, or recombining of things. Figuring out how a new technology could be used effectively in your organization constitutes an innovation. Taking a new approach to advertising your products or services is innovative. Revising employee schedules to increase shift coverage or to provide more flexibility constitutes a new idea. Any idea, when implemented to make your business more effective or profitable, constitutes an innovation in your organization. A new idea doesn't have to be new to the world, only a new approach in your organization.

So how and where do you get these ideas? I believe they come from some mysterious place in our subconscious that releases the idea when the right trigger presents itself. Actually, they often pop up when we least expect them. The harder you work at coming up with a new idea, the less likely you are to get one. Here are a few circumstances under which new ideas have come to me:

- In the shower—yes, ideas really do come to a lot of people there (It must be something in the water!)
- In or after dreams
- During quiet time when you really aren't thinking about anything
- From stray words picked up during incidental conversation

- While reading or listening to music
- In formal brainstorming sessions

Whatever your avenue, new ideas emerge uniquely from your perspective on the needs of the business. Ideas are distilled from your knowledge and experiences.

You have to take time to think to get a new idea.

In your organization, no one knows the work you perform the way you do. That means you are the best person to assess how things could be done better, faster, and more cost-effectively. Your knowledge, even if you share it with others, is a source of new ideas. Sometimes it's hard to accept that we are the organization's "experts" on how to do our jobs. In fact, it is our responsibility to "think" about what we do and how we do it in the context of the larger organization. We need to stay focused on how to improve the performance outcomes we impact. That's how success comes to us and our organization—through our implemented new ideas.

New ideas often flow from one to another. Once your thinking is opened up, it recognizes other opportunities for innovation. I have clients who have implemented new ideas of their own that have been instrumental in making their organizations better. Here are a few new ideas they have implemented successfully:

- Managing a corporate services work group like an independent consulting firm
- Running a nonprofit social service agency using business best practices

- Building a fitness studio as a community of the committed, not a gym
- Selling specialty products where aficionados meet rather than in a store
- Conducting a peer review of individual performance goals to build shared commitments

Implementing new ideas is a matter of taking a fresh look at the way things have always been done and seeing how you can do them better. Let's see how our cast of characters did with this public move.

Ideas Have a Power of Their Own

Our cast offers us examples of the power of innovation, on both sides of the coin.

Matt Clinger waited for direction from upper management; he wasn't an innovator. Why? Because he didn't like change. He liked the comfort of the processes and systems that he had followed for years. He didn't want the standards to change or his role, his approach, or his relationships. Consequently, he did not suggest initiatives unless he was instructed to and would frequently dismiss the ideas of others to avoid the change. You know where that got him.

Hal Dodger, on the other hand, became confused by new ideas because they disrupted his desire to operate in his own world. Hal did not want to work with others. He wanted to "do his own thing in his own way." When he didn't have the skills to perform effectively in his job, he was unable to come up with new ideas to realign his work style to new requirements. He wouldn't change the way he worked and resisted ideas from others to get himself out of his downward performance spiral. Hal is an important example of the need to be able to apply new ideas to yourself.

On the upside, Doug Hart was the kind of guy whose new ideas abounded. When he saw an opportunity to change his career, he took it. He wasn't stuck to the image he had of himself as a business major. He was open to the idea that he had the skills to be an OR technician. That led to the idea that he could transfer his hospital knowledge to medical equipment sales. Since then he's added new home construction and property management to his bag of tricks. Each of Doug's new ideas had its roots in business opportunity; his willingness to take risks has benefited his career and the organizations he's worked for.

Julia Masters was an incubator for new ideas, starting with her idea to make something of herself as a career woman by first completing her accounting degree. She then decided to expand her academic credentials to meet or exceed the requirements of the career moves that interested her. As she increased her knowledge expertise and the leadership skills to go with them, she saw endless opportunities to improve company processes, raise standards, and improve performance. In each new job, she presented her innovative ideas in the context of business best practices and then made them work. Julia is a prime example of how implementing new ideas has value both to you personally and to your organization.

The Cooks had a new idea—turn an old tavern into a gourmet restaurant. Then they took their collective talents for directing musical theatre and applied it to a dining experience with an entertainment flare. The Cooks knew food and used new ideas to create new menus and memorable dishes to keep their customers coming back. That's a pretty tasty success story.

Dr. Barker needed some new ideas to rebuild the morale of his practice employees. When he didn't know what to do himself, he sought out the consulting expertise he needed. Then he was willing to make changes in his leadership approach—that took real commitment. Initially, Dr. Barker didn't like coming to grips with the changes that were needed, and there were periods of resistance. But the desired improvements were so important to him, that he learned new skills, implemented new processes, increased his communication, arranged for some staff training, and reaped the benefits for years to follow.

In a Nutshell

Business fitness is a new idea. It's a new way of looking at the contributing factors of career success. You've read about the private moves and the public ones. You've followed the stories of real people who have succeeded or struggled to become business fit. Along the way, you have likely been assessing yourself to see if any of this works for you, if you can find the discipline to increase your business fitness, and if you can put the pieces together.

More than likely, there have been points along the way that you have resisted. You may be saying to yourself, "I can't do that in my organization." You know my answer: "Of course you can. You just need to be patient, come up with that new idea, that right idea, that you can implement when opportunity presents itself."

Implementing new ideas is the lifeblood of every business. Without new ideas, performance begins to wither. That's true for you as well. Without new ideas for thinking about and acting on your path to success, your progress will stall; you'll lose momentum and become discouraged. When you become discouraged, little by little you start to give up on your goals, lose your focus, and settle for something less than what you really want.

Business fitness is an outcome. You reach it by working on each of the private and public moves a little bit every day. Business fitness enhances your options for choice and choice positions you for success. The last chapter will take you home.

PUBLIC MOVES INVENTORY: IMPLEMENT NEW IDEAS

The third public move is to implement new ideas, using your business fitness to innovate initiatives that will enhance the business and your success potential. You need to be prepared to implement new ideas that are practical by identifying performance improvement needs and opportunities in your organization, using your following to test that idea, finding management support, and building an implementation plan. Use your responses here to identify new ideas and a plan to move them forward.

List three ideas that would improve performance in your organization. Then list the outcomes/benefits that would result from your idea.

Idea   **Outcomes/Benefits**

1.

2.

3.

For each idea above, list the names of people from your following willing/able to help flesh out a plan for your idea.

Idea   **Member of Your Following**

1.

2.

3.

For each idea above, list the change impacts that your idea will create. Now write your plan.

Idea   **Change Impacts**

1.

2.

3.

PART FOUR

LIFELONG SUCCESS

Chapter 11

BUSINESS FITNESS:
MAKING IT WORK—YOUR WAY

Now that you understand what it takes to achieve business fitness, it's time to start putting the pieces together in ways that work for you. After all, the whole point of becoming business fit is to position yourself to attain the success you want by maximizing your options.

Achieving business fitness is a process, not a regimen. It's organic, not linear. That means that you don't start with the first private move (stay well) and proceed through the next six moves one at a time, waking up one morning in a glorious state of business fitness. The reason why it doesn't work that way is because the steps are never complete—you work on all of them simultaneously all the time—sometimes consciously and other times subconsciously.

It's just like any workout program. You need to repeat those crunches or that jogging or those stretches to some degree every day or your physical fitness level will either never develop or start to decline. The concept of fitness implies a level of conditioning that is developed and increased incrementally until maximum desired performance is attained. Achieving business fitness and its success outcomes work the same way.

Each success is an elixir that excites you to do more.

Your business fitness, then, is always a work in progress. Although you are never done, you are always getting better. You are building your preparation and fueling your readiness. You are taking steps that create momentum, adding one invaluable experience to another, continuously expanding your insights and perceptions, building your capabilities like a well-balanced investment portfolio. Along the way you start to experience successes of all kinds and on all levels. The more successes you experience, the more willing you are to explore new opportunities and to take on new challenges.

The beauty of the seven business fitness moves is that they are transferable from one business to another, one community organization to another, and one professional specialty to another. The important thing to remember is that when you change organizations, you need to align each of your moves with the circumstances and people unique to that business. Each time you make a change, you will need to build new connections, to figure out how to stay current in a new field, and to attract a new following. You will also need to think about new ideas to implement that are suitable to the new organization. Once you develop a pattern of applying the private and public moves of business fitness, you will be able to put them to work wherever you are.

Your business fitness is a means to an end, not the end itself.

It is important to think about business fitness in the competitive world the way an athlete thinks of his or her physical fitness during a sports contest. The level of your fitness is what you draw on to come out on top. Sometimes we succeed and sometimes we don't. Each time a variable changes—the competition or the contest, the market or the playing field, the leadership or the coach—we change the conditions under which our fitness is tested. That's why we never achieve the ultimate in business fitness or physical fitness—we just keep working to position ourselves to be competitive enough to achieve the kind of success we desire in the end.

Sometimes Things Aren't What They Seem

You'll remember that from the time I was little, I had wanted to live on a farm and have horses. Where that idea came from is a bit sketchy, but somehow it was nestled in my psyche along with my Annie Oakley fantasy. I learned how to ride horses as an adult, spent ten years puttering around stables on my days off, and then decided to buy a small farm for the two horses I had come to own. Although I knew nothing about the technicalities of maintaining a farm or breeding horses, before too long I was running a commercial horse breeding operation.

My simplistic thinking was: "Hey, I've been successful in a big corporation. I understand the business model. I've developed a broad spectrum of business capabilities. Ergo, I'll just transfer my skills and knowledge to the horse breeding business." Needless to say, I was wrong on many levels. Why? Because the commercial horse breeding industry is not where I had been successful; it is a very high risk business with its roots in agriculture not energy production. Horse breeding is at the mercy of the uncontrollable laws and whims of nature, not government regulation. The product output of this business is contingent upon the successful or unsuccessful pregnancies of mares. It requires eleven months of waiting for a foal to be born without complications or death. There is no guarantee that even a healthy foal will have the appearance, temperament, or conformation desired by horse sport enthusiasts.

I was also naïve and uninformed about the unnerving "cost of goods" sold (what it really costs to get a mare pregnant, care for her until foaling, then raise and train the foal) and a horse sales and marketing system that can eat your lunch faster than you can say, "I'll have an order of fries with that."

To position myself for success in this business, I had to stay well because horses need care, stalls need cleaning, and farm chores need doing every day. I needed to stay focused on the bottom line (the ultimate success measure) because horses under your care without good market value will literally consume the profit from the others. I needed to stay current so I would know when to sell and when to wait; I needed to stay connected because it's those connections that make or break your position in the sales arena. (In this industry, every horse presented for sale is a "one of a kind" item sold on the basis of potential or past performance. In every case, you are selling a prospect for future performance success.) When I started my breeding business, once I got past "stay well," my business fitness was very shaky.

Once I had produced a few successful foals, I started to attract a following, albeit small. People who bought horses from me told their friends. But that process was painfully slow and sporadic. When sales markets got soft for one breed, I changed to another—implementing a new idea—and that created some limited success.

In spite of my love of the horses and the thrills that each foal brought, I realized that, after breeding commercially for fifteen years, this industry's business platform was not going to be a lifelong fit for me. I had thrown myself into a new enterprise without understanding its culture, its inner workings, or its codes. Did I have significant successes and failures? Yes. Will I always have horses with me at the farm? Of course. Did I learn invaluable lessons? Absolutely! Did this business experience increase my preparation and readiness for challenges in corporate roles and in consulting? Sure.

Would I do it again? Of course, but hopefully I'd be more business fit the next time.

I share this experience with you because too often success books sugarcoat things. They make these practices sounds so easy. Then when you tackle them and they don't go that smoothly, you become discouraged, feeling worse than you did before you started. There is no magic pill for achieving business fitness or success. It's about trying; you should always give yourself lots of points for that. When you try something and it doesn't work, try something else. What you never want to do is give up. When you give up, you don't learn anything and when that happens, you stall and lose momentum. Every positive thing and every negative thing that you experience along the way is knowledge that you will use to create a success the next time a similar situation presents itself.

To become business fit you have to work at it! You have to think about your life and come up with the new ideas that will take you where you want to go. You need to make changes even when they make you uncomfortable. (Hey, how scared do you think I was when I delivered my first foal alone in a cold, dark stall at 5 a.m.?) When you're afraid to do something, ask yourself what you would do if your own fear wasn't standing in the way. When you find yourself resisting a new opportunity or the need to step out of your comfort zone and make those private and public moves, find a way to overcome your fear. The seven business fitness moves give you a framework to follow so you can empower yourself to achieve the success you want for a lifetime.

Building a Business Fitness Plan

Getting started always seems to be the big challenge. Committing to becoming business fit is a change. You read about that in Chapter 10. Change disrupts the way you are currently doing things, so you will need to acknowledge first what you intend to do differently and commit to doing it no matter how much you'd like to stick with what you are doing now. When you have that urge, remind yourself that you are committed to your business fitness moves because you want to achieve a level of success that is *not* within your reach right now. If you don't change some things, you will stay where you are; if you do change some things, you will move forward toward what you want.

If you've been completing the business fitness inventories at the end of each chapter, you have essential information from which to put together your personal business fitness plan. Your plan should be goals-based with specific measures to help you assess your progress and build momentum. Your momentum and your motivation will be strongly linked to those measures. The measure is the way you keep score. That's how you know that you are making progress. So when you write your action plan, state the action steps as though they were performance goals: make them specific, measurable, attainable, realistic, and time driven. The most important measure is the date/month/quarter that you will complete that step. Remember: the more actions steps you complete, the more progress you are making.

It is impossible for me to prescribe a set of actions that will make you business fit. The business fitness moves are not a recipe—they are a process. How you achieve your business fitness is a product of what kind of success you want, where you are in terms of your preparation and readiness, what kind of momentum you want to generate, and the line of work you are currently in.

You should start by establishing what your success indicators are. In a sense this is like your personal mission statement. So please do not skip this step. (Reread Chapter 1 as a refresher.) Once you have a clear sense of your direction, then you can set goals around the actions that you believe will position you for success. A blank action template is provided in Appendix B.

Below is a sample action plan for someone who decides that a new job or a promotion is what they want. You would follow this same planning process for any other result you desired like starting your own business, re-credentialing yourself, or entering politics.

SAMPLE ACTION PLAN: MAKE A CAREER MOVE

Goals	Steps/Tasks
Find a more satisfying and better paying job by (date)	List the types of businesses that interest you
	List job titles preferred
	Research general salary/benefits ranges
	List knowledge, skills, and experience required
	Assess your capabilities against requirements
	Update résumé
	Talk with people connected with these jobs
	Explore career websites, newspapers, etc.
	Practice interviewing skills
	Apply for open positions

Get promoted by (date)	Identify positions of interest
	Study the knowledge and skill requirements of that position
	Talk with incumbents to learn about the position
	Talk with your supervisor about how to prepare for a promotion
	Prepare a development plan to enhance your credentials
	Make a specific plan that will showcase your capabilities in your current job
	Apply when the right jobs are posted

Your responses on Your Preparation and Readiness Inventory (Chapter 2) and Your Momentum Inventory (Chapter 3) will help you identify key actions that will drive your action plan.

The action plan defines the "game" you are in. Think of it like an athlete. Early in an athlete's career, the goal is to get selected for the team—any team. Then it's to convince the coach to make that athlete a starter. The ongoing goal is to participate on a team of higher and higher significance—high school, college, semi-pro, pro. Each accomplishment along the way positions that athlete for the next level of participation.

Your business fitness action planning is the way you build up your performance capital to position you for that next level of opportunity. You can also draw on your responses from the private and public moves inventories at the end of the chapters to build your action plan. Below are samples that will help you get started.

Sample Action Plans for
Each of the 7 Business Fitness Moves

STAY WELL	
Goal	**Steps/Tasks**
Reduce lost time from work due to illness by two days over the prior year	List causes of lost time from illness Build immunity: take a multivitamin and increase sleep by two hours nightly Increase daily exercise by doing ten minutes of stretches and/or walking for twenty minutes Spend at least fifteen minutes four days a week in the fresh air Be diligent about hand washing Add fresh fruits and vegetables to my daily diet

STAY FOCUSED	
Goal	**Steps/Tasks**
Write three work-life goals by (date) to complete this year and assess progress monthly	Spend at least twenty minutes of quiet time weekly over a three week period to think about my goals Then write specific goal statements for myself Share my three goals with a trusted friend or advisor; seek input and finalize Develop an action plan of the major results needed to achieve my goals Keep a log of the actions taken Each month review my goals, assess progress, and redirect activities

STAY CURRENT

Goal	Steps/Tasks
Read one business/ trade publication per week and read one business book per month (12 total)	List the publication and books that best promise to enhance my knowledge Read the periodical in hard copy or on-line Read or listen to the books Keep articles and/or take notes on information for future reference; file these Keep a list of my reading

STAY CONNECTED

Goal	Steps/Tasks
Keep in touch with a minimum of four professional contacts each month (48 total for the year)	Make a list of professional contacts Contact one person each week for a phone conversation, meeting, lunch, or correspondence Keep track of the commitments I make to each person Deliver on what I commit Keep a list of those contacted and the outcome

ATTRACT A FOLLOWING

Goal	Steps/Tasks
Increase recognition of my technical or job knowledge with at least one supervisor, client, or customer by (date)	Identify the area of knowledge that represents my expertise
	Make a list of the people who would benefit from my knowledge
	Make a list of opportunities where I can share my knowledge
	Prepare a document of helpful information for others
	Offer to coach, mentor, or assist someone needing my knowledge
	Offer to participate on a team where my knowledge will be useful
	Ask for feedback on how satisfied they were with my contributions
	Ask how I could have been more helpful
	Keep in contact with the people with whom I worked

TAKE THE LEAD

Goal	Steps/Tasks
Become the single point of contact for a key customer (internal or external) by (date)	Determine who my customers are
	Identify a customer need that I could fill by becoming a single point of contact
	Discuss my interest in this role with my supervisor
	Meet with the customer and develop a mutually satisfactory working relationship

Develop the processes and
communication needed to support
my customer
Serve the customer and ask for
feedback
Report results to my supervisor

IMPLEMENT NEW IDEAS

Goal	Steps/Tasks
Improve a key business/ administrative process for my work area	Identify the weaknesses in an existing process and its impact on the business
	Map a new process that delivers more effectiveness and cost benefit
	Review the new process with the appropriate people
	Offer to field test my proposed process
	Oversee full implementation
	Offer to perform a process effectiveness assessment after thirty days
	Report findings and suggest next steps

As you can see, the goals you set will require focused action and commitment. The broader and more complex the goal, the more work it will require. But remember:

**Business fitness, like your life,
is not a race—it is an unfolding.**

For each goal you set for yourself, work on it one step at time. In the examples here, I loaded them so that you can see how many approaches, steps, and options you could undertake. Your challenge is to manage the development of your business fitness along with the other demands on your life. That requires balance and discipline.

If you are reading this part and saying, "This is just too hard," that can't be. How can something be too hard if YOU are the one designing it? This is about *your* business fitness, *your* success plan, and *your* future. You are in charge. These are your choices. No one is evaluating your progress other than you. If you recall, four of the seven moves are private. You don't need to share your goals or plans with anyone if you don't want to. But if you do, share them with someone who will be your champion—someone who wants you to achieve a level of success that fits you.

Business fitness is about the power to succeed *your* way. We all start small and simply. The more success we experience, the more we will take on. Sometimes we make great strides and other times we feel stuck. When that happens, you just pull your feet out of the mud and take one more step. The road to business fitness mirrors the road to physical fitness—one exercise repetition at a time. You are fully capable of taking charge of your work life and finding the success that you want. Your commitment to achieving business fitness gives you the power to make the right things happen. If you really want to, you will.

APPENDIX A

SKILLS AND KNOWLEDGE INVENTORY

What you can do and what you know are key elements to your business fitness. You can use this skills and knowledge inventory to help you stay focused on what you need to do to keep yourself prepared and ready to move your business life forward.

Below is a partial list of skills important to success in any business. Make a note of the skills that you already have and want to use throughout your work life. Then mark the ones that you need to develop. Keep adding to the list as additional skill needs surface. Then build a list of the content knowledge that you bring to your work or want to develop. There are some examples offered here to get you started.

These skills and knowledge terms are the language of business. The more aware you are of how to use this language and apply it in the workplace, the more effective you will be building your business fitness.

Skills (Things you can do)	Knowledge (Content matter that you know)
Product/services sales	*Examples:*
Product/services marketing	Microsoft Office applications
Strategy planning	Urban planning
Team building	Property tax law
Goal setting/attainment	Early childhood education
Communication:	Electrical engineering
Oral	Public accounting
Written	Retailing and merchandising
Listening	
Data analysis	
Problem analysis	
Action planning	
Motivating others	
Partnering	
Relationship building	
Model development	
Financial analysis	
Networking	
Market analysis	
Organizing	
Leadership	
Decisiveness	
Innovation	
Abstract reasoning	
Initiative	
Interpersonal relations	
Cost control	

Budgeting
Big picture thinking
Consulting
Training
Solutions integration
Customer service
Time management
Hiring/selection
Leveraging
Business development
Employee/personnel development
Program development
Creativity
Process improvement
Troubleshooting
Vendor management
Outsourcing
Self-management/self-starting
Recruitment
Tolerance for ambiguity
Influencing
Negotiations
Contracting
Message packaging
Presentation skills
Managing multiple priorities

ACTION PLAN TEMPLATE

Instructions:

Make copies of this template and use them to build your business fitness action plan as described in Chapter 11. You'll see that this version of the template encourages you to identify the reasons why you are ahead or behind on your goals and to keep track of what you are learning along the way. What you learn—both on the upside and downside—help you to stay committed to actions that will get you where you want to go.

GOAL	STEPS/TASKS	COMPLETE BY DATES	REASONS AHEAD/BEHIND	LESSONS LEARNED/ COMMITMENTS